Breathing Patterns

Breathing Patterns

A Teacher's Reflections on Calling, Equipping, and Sending

Robert P. Hoch

WIPF & STOCK · Eugene, Oregon

BREATHING PATTERNS
A Teacher's Reflections on Calling, Equipping, and Sending

Copyright © 2010 Robert P. Hoch. All rights reserved. Except for brief quotations in critical publications or reviews, no part of this book may be reproduced in any manner without prior written permission from the publisher. Write: Permissions, Wipf and Stock Publishers, 199 W. 8th Ave., Suite 3, Eugene, OR 97401.

Wipf & Stock
An Imprint of Wipf and Stock Publishers
199 W. 8th Ave., Suite 3
Eugene, OR 97401

www.wipfandstock.com

ISBN 13: 978-1-60608-526-4

Manufactured in the U.S.A.

*Dedicated to the students of
the University of Dubuque Theological Seminary*

Contents

Foreword by Jana Childers / ix

Acknowledgements / xiii

Introduction / 1

PART ONE: CALLING / 11
   1 People of the Penguin / 23
   2 Travel Advisories / 30
   3 Mercy on Thin Ice / 38
   4 The Day after Christmas / 46
   5 Our Greatest Possession / 52

PART TWO: EQUIPPING / 59
   6 The Most True Thing / 67
   7 Learning to Pray in August / 75
   8 Staying On until Pentecost / 84
   9 Nothing, Nada, Zip! / 91
   10 Working with Clay / 97

PART THREE: SENDING / 105
   11 Looking for Someone to Blame / 122
   12 Dancing in the Desert / 129
   13 Casting Shadows / 137
   14 Breathing Patterns / 143
   15 Sound of Sirens / 150

Bibliography / 157

Foreword

A HEART FOR THE displaced and dispossessed, an ability to see beauty in the broken, these have long been hallmarks of Rob Hoch's preaching. Compassion is not an abstract quality to Rob, as the sermons and essays found here make clear. His words teem with image and poetic lyric, ribbons and riffs of heart language play across the page. He points out the mystery "that does not dissolve before the acids of theoretical explanation," describes the disciples' "manic fear," and wonders whether the relationship between seminary and church is "bipolar". He pictures a parent trying to help an active child cross the street, saying it is "like (having) a thirty pound frog tethered to your arm."

In the sermons and essays which comprise these pages prophetic texts make their "ear-piercing, heart-racing way straight into the place where we live." Fresh metaphors provoke (will the sickness that plagues theological education turn out to be like that of a woman who is having a difficult pregnancy?) and word play delights (who knew the name of the rich man who encounters Jesus in Mark 10 was "Richie"?). The deft use of refrain thrills: "If you take that journey, you take that chance" sings through a sermon. The chances are well worth taking here. In these pages we enter a land where images pop with emotion and prompt reflection.

Reading these sermons leaves no doubt that this Presbyterian pastor, this man of Athabascan and German ancestry, this daddy of small girls and teacher of preachers feels for and with his listeners. His sermons are full of uncanny insights—the kind that arise from a deep capacity for empathy. Identification with the dispossessed and with the listener are skills many preachers struggle to develop. It almost seems like Rob was born with them.

But this volume is about more than heart-touching sermons—more than the imagistic, imaginative sermons for which Rob is known. Over and over again in these pages, are substantial examples of what the much bally-hood "integration" looks like in preaching. Integrating a lively mind with a tender heart is not as easy as it may sound. Most preachers lean more heavily to one side than the other. But Rob plays it straight down the middle, holding together in his affections image and idea, cerebrum and cerebellum, classroom and sanctuary.

This is one reason his sermons breathe and fly. They are full of air—of the kind of oxygen that is generated by honoring all sides of the human experience and treating the ambiguity one finds there with respect. Reality is not simplified here. There are some blacks and whites, but the shades of gray abound. Complexity is not neatly resolved. Questions hang in the air. What is "community"? Is there too much "distance" in residential education? Does "distance education" allow for formation? What role does "community" play in nurturing faith?

Perhaps the author is able to hold these things together precisely because they are held together in him. He looks at the complicated issues of faith and education unflinchingly because he is able to look at himself that way. Humility makes him able to tell his own stories even as it keeps him from telling too much. TMI is not a failing of Rob Hoch's. He has a deft touch for using a snapshot of his own life to stir a deep spot in the listener.

Rob's ability to stir with language reminds me of the very first sermon he ever preached. As the slightly green instructor in his Introduction to Preaching class, I was perhaps a bit underprepared to deal with the quiet young poet on the back row. Two days before he was to preach, he submitted his manuscript, as the course syllabus required. As I read it, my heart sank. Before my eyes, line on line and page on page of poetry unfolded. It did not look like any first-sermon I had ever seen before. It did not, in fact, look like any sermon manuscript I'd ever seen. As I leafed through the pages, my red pen drooping above the desk, I made an agonizing decision, "I'm going to have to speak to him face to face about this," I thought. When the innocent-looking student answered the summons to my office I took the bull by the horns. "Rob," I blurted out, "I am sorry if I wasn't clear, but the point of the assignment was for you to use your own words in the sermon. It is just not acceptable to submit one of the long poems of T.S. Eliot." The young man looked at me concerned, his face pale and, if anything, yet more innocent. "Professor," he replied, "those are my words. All of them." All of them were indeed Rob's words. It had never once crossed my mind that they could be anybody but Eliot's. But they were. They were the words of another one of God's great poets. One who was destined to fill the pulpit and the classroom with beautiful word pictures. To make listeners think and readers ponder. To make us all feel something of God's compassion breathing in us.

Jana Childers
San Francisco Theological Seminary

Acknowledgements

While this book bears my name as its author, it would be more accurate to say that it has many authors, or better yet, many companions. Writing may be a lonely exercise but thinking, it seems to me, is impossible without the generous support of a community, a community diverse in region as well as in time. Because of this, thanksgiving is always partial and my debt to companions, ongoing.

Scholarship, of course, does not happen by accident. A community that values scholarship makes space for it to continue. In that spirit, I want to thank the President of the University of Dubuque Theological Seminary, Rev. Dr. Jeffrey Bullock and the Board of Trustees who generously supported a semester long sabbatical during which I developed the outlines of this project. And the Rev. Dr. Bradley Longfield, Dean of the Seminary, deserves credit for suggesting the idea of a collection of sermons. My colleagues on the faculty supplied a generous, collegial, and supportive engagement of the manuscript itself during one of our faculty forums. To each and all go my heartfelt thanks.

My colleagues here at the University of Dubuque Theological Seminary will also recognize their more informal contributions to this text, made up of conversations, questions and passions we have shared along the way, as well as spaces, including classroom, chapel, and church. Students, of course, were present when many of these sermons were born: they were in Blades Chapel, listening and responding with generosity and intelligence. Without the spirit of inquiry as well as the heart of passion that sustains seminarians these words would be empty indeed.

Two individuals should be singled out since they helped me "hear" this project in some of its earlier versions. Frank Hartzell, a life-long friend and conversation partner, brought an "off-the-grid" intelligence to this project, hearing as a person who has been loved by compassion and grace into Christ's church. Another long-time friend, Dr. Michael Hegeman, helped me along as well, bringing his warmth, keen eye, and scholarship to these sermons and reflections.

David Lott, who edited the final draft of the manuscript, supplied not only revisions but also sensitivity and care for the project itself.

A word of thanks also goes to Loretta Waughtal, seminary student and research assistant, who helped with the finishing touches on this manuscript by organizing the bibliography.

And finally, to my daily companions: our two daughters, Gwendoline and Imogen, and my wife and best friend, Rebecca. You break bread with me each day. I am always and happily in your debt.

Introduction

STREWN ACROSS THE FLOOR of my study are books that you might expect to see in a homiletician's workspace, books bearing titles like *Recovering Paul's Mother Tongue, Living Through Pain, On Job, Performance in Preaching*, and more like these, all signs of theological study and scholarship for the church. Occasionally, however, another sort of book might be mixed in among the more predictable titles. On one occasion, it happened to be a copy of Kevin Henkes's *Lilly's Purple Plastic Purse*, boasting a picture of Lilly the Mouse dancing through the air, sporting some very cool sunglasses, wearing garish red cowboy boots, and, yes, holding aloft the infamous purple plastic purse that plays a cute little jingle whenever she opens it. Not surprisingly, that oversized, unapologetically loud, totally unscholarly text seemed to draw attention to itself. The sight of Lilly the Mouse, heaped among the other more respectable titles, generated a bit of friendly ribbing from my seminary colleagues: "*Lilly's Purple Plastic Purse*, eh? Is that the kind of reading you homileticians do? Glad to see you're keeping up with cutting-edge scholarship!"

I sometimes felt the urge to cover it up, bury it under something respectable like Brevard Childs's *Isaiah*, or hide it beneath a pile of ungraded papers, where I knew I could find it quickly if I needed to, but well out of sight. But for some reason I chose to keep it where it was, right there on the floor, competing with the other books, respectable or not. In the end, I was glad for my hesitancy, not only because of the good laugh it generated among the faculty, laughter I enjoyed, but because of my daughters' reactions when, one day, they opened the door to my study.

As it happened, I had just returned to the office when they opened the door, and with a sideways glance I saw them looking aghast at the mess on my floor, worse than any mess they had ever created in the playroom of our home. But once they recovered from their shock, I got a quick admonishment from our three-year-old daughter, Imogen, who pointed to my floor, spitting out an indignant "Clean this up!" And then, a second or two later, they saw *their* book, the one we read at home, tossed among the other "serious" adult books that interest them not a whit. For her part, Gwendoline, five years old, generously allowed that I could "borrow" it for as long as I needed it; she was genuinely pleased that a book she loved had found its way into my world, with its crazy constellation of theological titles that often—too often—take me away from their company. If no one else viewed my reading as important, informative, and inspiring, Gwendoline surely did. To her, the sight of *Lilly's Purple Plastic Purse* in my office was nothing short of a confirmation of her exceptionally fine scholarship, not to mention a promising sign for her otherwise hopeless dad.

That experience suggests for me an image that may help name some of the tensions that surface occasionally between theological education and the church. While I would not want to overdraw the analogy, it does seem that the language of the church and the language of the seminary can interact in incongruous ways, such that the language of the church, when it shows up in the seminary, can seem rather like spying a children's book in a theologian's study. Somehow the juxtaposition of the two strikes us as curious, and perhaps laughable, as if one did not belong in the company of the other. And yet, for a child, nothing could lend more confirmation to their sense of experience and wisdom than to see this kind of book occupying the otherwise remote space of a theologian's study. As I think about it, the sight of a children's book in my study probably did more for our daughters' perception of theological inquiry than theological inquiry itself will ever do.

I suppose I need to clarify what I do *not* intend by this analogy. I do not intend to describe a "hierarchy" of knowledge, where the church engages in "silly" stories and the seminary only attends to substantive thought. Even spending a short season with children's books exposes the readers to vast wisdom, often poetically expressed, and always communally shared. Among the titles that come to mind are Maurice Sendak's *Where the Wild Things Are*, or Hans Christian Anderson's *The Emperor's New Clothes*, or John Steptoe's *The Story of Jumping Mouse*—from the exploration of the subtle paradoxes between wilderness and domesticity, to the prophetic clarity of a child's voice, to the dramatic chronicling of Jumping Mouse's transformation into Eagle, each of these stories betrays a depth that theologians would rightly envy for their own writing. At the same time, neither do I intend to make light of sustained theological inquiry and its place in the life of the church. As a discipline, theological study demands much from us, often more than we are either able or willing to give. Perhaps more to the point, we might think of the yields of theological reflection that appear (we hope) in the mission and witness of the church.

And, of course, that expression of uncertainty ("we hope") begs the question: Just how does the seminary relate to the life of the church? Where, if at all, do we see the congruency between the mission of seminary and the mission of the local church? How do they inform each other through shared dialogue and a shared sense of vocation? And perhaps more pressing, how might the contemporary ecologies of church and society be reshaping the experience of theological education, for better or worse? Do the contemporary crises facing mainline denominations and institutions of theological education create an opportunity for constructive visioning of today's church and its relationship to the classroom?

Having read this introduction and, now, these questions, you might expect the body of this book to be a linear exposition of the problem and its solution. That might be a book for another day. As for *this* book, made up of sermons and more extended meditations on the themes of calling, equipping, and sending, my goal finds expression in something more basic: I believe the connection between the church and seminary appears most starkly in the event of chapel worship, something we need to remember, particularly during a time of exilic self-examination. Weekday chapel serves as a vital link between church and classroom. Within the context of a community of scholars and students at worship, we see a remarkable event of coming together, sometimes appearing almost like a reconciliation between church and classroom. At other times, worship brings a note of remembrance to the classroom. And not uncommonly, chapel worship supplies an exciting synthesis of disparate areas of inquiry, bringing the fruits of scholarship into space we share with the church. Relatedly, it would seem that the classroom, a space never far removed from chapel, forms an important context or metaphor for reflection on the continuing reform of church and classroom alike.

Expressed another way, seminary community finds its formation not just through the classroom or through our respective disciplines, but through weekday worship in seminary chapel. The chapel, a place where seminarians and professors "interrupt" the business of the classroom to participate in Word and Sacrament, suggests an "intersection" and, as such, a locus for theological reflection on our collective vocation. Viewed in this light, chapel looks something like a "middle ground" between church and classroom. But this conception does not quite get at things, not exactly. Something ironic appears in the sense that the classroom never really disappears—putting it more strongly, the classroom is constituted first and foremost through the community at worship, being clothed in the language and manner of the church.

Just so, we enter the classroom, clothed in the narratives and patterns of Christian worship. Indeed, the classroom is composed not just of teachers and students; the spirit of the classroom also bears the memory of a community at worship, bathing our more critical work with the memory of our common baptism. The way classes dissolve into a journey to chapel, and chapel in turn dissolves into a journey back to class—professors and students walking in a leisurely manner to and from a service of worship—introduces a different dynamic to the classroom, creating, in the best tradition of theological education, a learning environment, for student and professor alike. Fostering that close connection adds an element of "recognition" to the experience of classroom instruction, reducing the sense of drift between church and classroom. Students and professors alike renew the life of worship as constitutive of our labor within the classroom.

So, while a difference exists between classroom and worship space, we would be wise not to impose too sharp a boundary between them. The title for this collection, *Breathing Patterns*, reflects that conviction: the relationship between theological reflection and pastoral vocation is as breath to speech or as sound to words. The one does not get very far, or even exist, without the other. But if we wanted to accentuate the place of worship relative to the classroom, stressing the priority of the former, we could say that the seminary classroom speaks with the accent of our common life in worship. Whether as teachers or students, when we gather in the classroom, we gather in response to the God who calls us. As Geoffrey Wainwright reminds us: ". . . [T]he theologian is truly theologian when, in his [or her] very theologizing, he [or she] is listening for the 'echo of a voice' and is contributing, even if indirectly, to the human praise of God. It is indeed a traditional dictum in Eastern Christianity that the true theologian is the theologian who prays."[1]

For the sake of reflection, we could also reverse Wainwright's insight, observing that a person of prayer *becomes* one who theologizes. Viewed

1. Wainwright, *Doxology*, 21.

this way, theology may appear less the domain of specialists than the natural outcome of the life of faith. The classroom, it turns out, forms a natural habitat for those who pray. Gerhard O. Forde suggests something along these lines as he draws the distinction between *talking about theology* and *being a theologian*:

> Things happen. Accidents. Tragedies. Deaths and funerals. Natural disasters. Illness. Loss. Suffering. Disappointment. Wrongdoing. And so on and on. There is also good fortune. . . . Experience of great beauty or pleasure. Sheer grace. Chance encounters that determine our lives. Love. We begin to wonder. God pops into our thinking and conversation. We may cry out in agony, "Why God?" or in relief, "Thank God!" Or we may just use God's name in cursing. Sooner or later we are likely to get thinking about God and wondering if there is some logic to it all in our lives, or some injustice. We become theologians.[2]

The primary language of faith comes out of these happenings, events that evoke from us outbursts of either wonder, or agony, or gratitude. Yet, these events, whether grief-stricken sighs or unanticipated outbursts of doxological praise, yearn for explanation, further reflection, and deeper examination. They do not *end* reflection but, in fact, *inaugurate* the questioning work of theological inquiry.

Somewhere between the inarticulate sigh and "being theologians" there is an event of hearing, of seeing Jesus amid these things, above these things, through these things, in these things. Perhaps one could say that preaching within the chapel space acts a bit like a midwife to the seminary classroom, coaxing and wooing our inchoate cries into faltering speech and then, crucially, into unending praise. The murmuring songs of worship and reflection are never very far removed from the labors and trials we experience in the classroom. This, of course, raises the question of context.

The truism that there is no such thing as a "universal sermon" applies to this collection of sermons, no less than any other. Most of the sermons in this collection were intended for the seminary community. Four, however, were intended for local congregations, which deserves a word of explanation. Initially, when I imagined this project, I thought a straightforward collection of seminary sermons would suffice, as if to say, "This is what happens in seminary chapel—doesn't that look famil-

2. Forde, *On Being a Theologian of the Cross*, 10–11.

iar?" However, while there are points of continuity with what happens in congregational worship, there are also differences that actually help us to keep in view the distinct but still closely related missions of seminary and church. Even when professors preach in chapel, our vision never strays far from the local congregations that our students will eventually pastor. These communities, and not the "temporary" setting of chapel, shape the character of our chapel rhetoric. One could almost say that seminary "borrows" preaching from the church such that, no matter how deeply invested we may be in the seminary community or academic discipline, we, too, speak from the pulpit, table, and baptismal font.

And sermons, unlike so many of those books piled on my office floor, express the oral/aural dynamic of preaching. Whereas for much of our academic lives, professors and students were formed in an educational environment of solitary study, our thoughts locked into the silence of a page, in our life as members of the church we were formed through the spoken word. This is the case here, as well, each sermon having attained its most appropriate expression as sound for the ear rather than as print for the page. As a consequence, some of the sermons will "read" better than others. Still, even as I *read* them, I *hear* them, recalling the "music" or "pitch" that I attempted to find within each message. I suppose that fact, the musicality of language, cadence, rhythm, and persona, expresses a distinctive feature of chapel preaching, especially as it returns the classroom to the first language of worship, reminding the seminary community that the word we study is more fittingly sung than merely examined. If we examine it, and we ought to, our examination best arises from our loving communion with it, a song we remember singing as we gathered together, the "song" guiding our study.

But the way a sermon *sounds*, its aural quality, moves us to think about those who first heard the message to begin with. As Fred Craddock points out, "[O]ne seldom hears the inquiry, Who heard his sermon? Almost always the question is, Who preached this sermon? in spite of the fact that a sermon has many ears but only one mouth."[3] So, to provide some description of those who heard these sermons: the "ears" for these sermons consisted of students, faculty, administrators, seminary staff, and sometimes immediate family or visitors. I hope you, the reader, hear

---

3. Craddock, *Preaching*, 31.

an echo of the rituals, symbols, rites of passage, and values that form a seminary community's preoccupations and passions.

The act of hearing implies a certain posture or attitude. One listens differently to a lecture than one listens to a sermon or a poem or a newscast. The act of listening responds, in part, to the form of communication as well as the context of communication, among other variables. Likewise, the same could be said of the community that gathers for worship in chapel: they listen in unique ways, adopting postures appropriate to setting, medium, and message. So, we might ask, How does a seminary community listen? In what ways, if any, does that act of listening differ from a congregation's similar act of listening on the Lord's Day? From one vantage point, the way a seminary community listens does not differ dramatically from that of a congregation on the Lord's Day. People attend to the reading of Scripture and to its proclamation; they listen with a sense of anticipation; they listen to be shaped, to be fed, and to be pastored through the proclaimed word. Many of those who attend chapel might describe their worship as an expression of their spiritual discipline, an explanation similar to the one laypeople might use when talking about their worship practices.

And yet, the dynamic relationship between chapel and classroom does introduce something of a paradox to our attitude in chapel worship. That dynamic underscores a basic and valuable tension between classroom and chapel space, something we begin to get at by looking at the geographic and chronological relationship between chapel and classroom. A student, for example, walks perhaps two or three minutes from his or her classroom to the chapel service at 9:30 a.m. What happens as he or she walks across campus? Likely as not, she may be thinking about an assignment or sighing in relief, having just completed a midterm exam. He sees other students heading in the same direction, leaving campus, or skipping chapel in order to study. Likewise, he or she sees professors, their classes and study interrupted, making their way to chapel—or not. For those who attend chapel, after a thirty-minute service, the community shares fellowship briefly before returning to classes. During the day, it will not be too surprising to hear a reference to the chapel service in a classroom conversation, or in the hallway as students make their way through a grueling academic program. These patterns, even when people "skip" chapel, suggest a normative practice that keeps the classroom in close proximity to the life of worship, extending the interpretive life shared in chapel to the classroom, on an almost daily basis.

Yet a significant distance exists as well, mostly expressed as the difference between cultures. Almost invariably, people view chapel as an intrusion, whether they welcome it or refuse it. If they welcome it, it is a happy intrusion, one they greet with open arms. Indeed, some open their arms quite literally, waving their arms like fronds in the wind. If the preacher makes an especially wise observation, deserving of some "cluck" of community approbation, someone might cry out, "Amen!" or, more likely here in the Midwest, there would be a collective, barely audible guttural sound that you never hear in the classroom. Others, less happily, resent chapel's tendency to take up valuable time that could be used to prepare for class or exams. If they go to chapel, they walk in late, look at their watch during the sermon, sing a hymn if and only if they like it, and, if possible, duck out early.

Of course, another distance exists in terms of identification. It is almost never the case that those who elect to skip chapel object to worship per se. While there are usually some in a seminary community who, for reasons of their own, are not active in a local congregation, the vast majority of people in seminary do affiliate with a local congregation and worship regularly. *No one, however, is a member of chapel.* The sacrament of baptism is reserved to the local congregation that admits new members into the life of the church. That sacrament cements identity with a congregation, more deeply than a chapel can or ever should. Indeed, while it is relatively common to "remember" our baptism in chapel, it is rare, though not unheard of, to administer the sacrament of baptism in a seminary chapel. One could say that although chapel occurs frequently and within earshot of each member of the community, chapel has an almost "second-string" quality to it, a nice option for those who want it or need it, but not a requirement. The upshot of this is that our listening may be less a function of our identification with the tradition of the pulpit and more a function of our commitment to seminary community and its worship life.

Even so, I suspect that cultural differences between classroom and chapel introduce the most decisive distance of all. Whether happy or unhappy, present or absent, both attitudes express the sense that chapel does not quite "fit" into the culture of the classroom. The classroom, it turns out, provides the day-to-day context for chapel, constantly reminding the community of its very real work. But on its best days, chapel reminds the seminary community, including its classrooms, of its vocation: remembering our baptism, proclaiming God's word, hoisting the cup of salvation, proclaiming Christ's death until he comes.

While "distant" at some levels, chapel worship often deepens our sense of calling, giving depth to understanding, resonance to speech, and wisdom to learning. Someone says, "Thank you, today's worship helped me put Greek in perspective!"; or there in chapel, in the middle of the week, between meetings and exams, someone sheds a few quiet tears before gathering books and bag, making his way to class; or perhaps it is the feeling of community, being together, not being so terribly alone, our singing voices a sacramental confirmation of God's promise to be with us, always; or someone testifies, and we hear her voice, and in her voice, we hear God speaking, summoning us to a different way.

As we return to our classrooms, we return with an accent, our speech lilting with peculiar-sounding praise.

Patterns, breathing patterns, *calling, equipping,* and *sending*—these words bring to mind some of the patterns of discipleship that contribute to our larger vocations in the church and seminary and, as such, form recurring thematic patterns in chapel preaching. They also seem to serve nicely as a way of organizing this collection of sermons and my reflections on them. For each sermon, I offer some of what my thoughts were in preparing them, sometimes reflecting pastorally and, at other times, speaking more in the vein of theological scholarship.

A final word, perhaps an apology. Sermon collections sometimes seem to have an almost museum-like quality, as they are snatched out of context, plunked into a bottle of homiletical formaldehyde, and thereby preserved as specimens of a certain kind of preaching. Such collections always look depressing, like sad, soft figments of their former selves. An archivist confirmed this anxiety, as he talked about the relative value of an archived collection of sermons I was studying. He said they were little more interesting than historical artifacts and less interesting than history. The archivist expressed, so far as I can tell, a pretty broadly held view of sermons: they are for a time. And perhaps these sermons, too, are for a time. But I suppose it is what they *do* in their time that is finally more important than their time itself.

My own sense of the "doing" of these sermons is included in the meditations I offer on the topics of calling, equipping, and sending. In the process of writing, they evolved into reflections on what it means to "be" or "do" the theology of the cross in the church today, particularly in a time of crisis. Indeed, it strikes me that the title for this collection, *Breathing Patterns*, contains an ironic note, since many of the *patterns* of church life and theological education, patterns that we inherited from a previous generation, are in turmoil. We may still be breathing as churches and institutions of higher learning, but it is ragged breathing, the patterns indicative of institutional and missional health difficult to discern. We look for a pulse, a pattern of regularity, only to find palpitations, arrhythmias, and other disruptive signals from the vital organs of our body politic. The symbols that constitute narratives of discipleship are in turmoil, our manner of speech not as easy to identify as it was a generation ago.

But if that is the case, it does not follow that we no longer have a narrative or that the narrative we have been shaped by is lost. Far from it. God speaks and *ex nihilo*, out of nothing, creates worlds. Perhaps part of our vocation as preachers is to attempt to put into words the worlds God creates or is about to create, so that the church might "see Jesus" in ways renewing and transforming. In that sense, preaching resembles prayer, listening for the intercessory activity of the Spirit in proclamation. When we move one step from the act of preaching to the process of reflecting on preaching—that is, the theology of preaching—we discover the art of listening for the "'echo of a voice'"[4] in the act of proclamation. As I journeyed through these sermons, reflecting on the activity of proclamation, it seemed as if I were listening to an echo, trying to detect in it a theological range, an emphasis, a pastoral concern that animated a particular interpretation of text and context. Reading and rereading these sermons, I found their moment of witness shaping the theological story that continues to evolve in my own intellectual journey. I say "story" because I easily lapse into the partial and often fragmentary speech of poetry. I admire those who can speak in a manner more exhaustive than my own way of speaking, which sometimes seems like soulful limping. Limping or not, I hope that within these theological fragments, you will detect the "echo" of a community that preaches and teaches with the cadence of prayer.

---

4. Wainwright, *Doxology*, 21.

PART ONE

CALLING

I

And Jesus said to them,
"Follow me and I will make you fish for people."
And immediately they left their nets
and followed him.
(Mark 1:17–18)

WALKING INTO THE SEMINARY building on our campus, you immediately encounter a display case containing an assortment of items, seemingly random and unrelated; they might look curious, strangely left behind, perhaps appearing somewhat like the shoreline of the Sea of Galilee might have to a passerby after Jesus called the first disciples, its shore littered with abandoned nets, fishing gear, empty boats, as well as a few bewildered parents. While there are not many nets on this midwestern shore, one does get a sense of what students have left behind as they made their way to seminary: there's a child's drawing of a girl in a green dress, wearing a princess crown, a pink flower held in her right hand, and a note at the bottom in the careful handwriting of a preschooler: "To: Christine." On the other side of the case, you see a beadwork necklace, displaying Nez Perce colors and symbols, an eagle occupying the middle of a large circular pendant. From there, your eyes might drop to the lower part of the case, where you would notice business cards and licenses, documents, symbols of skills and credentials, dropped like leaves to the ground. Another flyer bears photos of a modest, well-looked-after home, a "For Sale" sign posted on its front lawn. Someone else has filled a glass vial with soil from Montana, earth from a place once called home. The shores of seminaries are littered with memories, bits of life, symbols, authorities, skills, relationships, lands, and peoples—left behind but perhaps not entirely forgotten.

When I was a boy, we sometimes went to an abandoned cannery town on the Eyak River, near Cordova, Alaska. Devastated by the 1964 earthquake, this particular village was left landlocked, effectively ending its role in the once-thriving fishing industry of the Prince William Sound. On weekends, my stepfather would take us there, up the river in an airboat, skimming over water and land almost like they were the same thing, the roar of the engine overpowering the wax my mother stuffed into our ears in a vain attempt to preserve our hearing. But when the engine idled down, finally going silent, there was no sound at all except the visible echoes of someone's yesterday: dishes still in the cupboard; a dining-room table surrounded by upended chairs; labels for canned salmon scattered on the floor; a salt shaker in the shape of a teddy bear, its gold enamel worn to white from use at table; rooms where the floorboards creaked, and homes where paint peeled and windows were broken; abandoned walkways, forgotten docks, and the quiet way of the river.

II

They say a place never quite leaves you. And if you leave it, you will always bear its memory, a peculiar ache difficult to explain.

Difficult to explain, it may well be, but it is almost commonplace in today's culture of displacement, an experience which, according to some, is among the defining characteristics of the modern age: "War, mass expulsion, famine, environmental degradation, human rights violations, and fear of oppression have sent millions upon millions of men, women, and children into exile."[1] Ours, we are told, is the age of the refugee.[2] A refugee community: forced out of homes, into camps or reservations, into

---

1. Merrill, *The Old Bridge*, 6.
2. Ibid., 6.

the anonymity of the inner city or the homogeneity of the suburbs, out of our cultural skins not by choice but just to survive. Among survivors, the memory of place persists, something like the way Jadranka, a Bosnian refugee from the Balkan war, describes her people's experience of exile:

> They're like people who have lost a limb. Amputees. They can still feel their homeland, even though it's gone. It tingles. Subconsciously they know everything was destroyed, but as long as they're in a camp they can dream it's still there. Those who integrate into society know they'll never go back, those in camps all believe they will return.[3]

An amputee: a person known to the world, and perhaps even to oneself, by the character of his or her disfigurement.

The comparison may seem peculiar, thinking of calling as an experience of the displaced, but there is something about it that holds. To be sure, there are differences. Those who enter seminary respond to God's call freely, unlike a refugee community driven from its home by alien forces. Even when students come from a Native community, the "rez" for example, or out of the persecution experienced by African Christians in the Sudan, they do so as an expression of hope and not as a surrender to despair. Nevertheless, a called community carries with it a memory of a place and a people, often a people for whom disfigurement is not marginal but, rather, primary to its experience. More pointedly, and reaching all of us with fearful consequence, it remains that we who are called are summoned by Christ *and* his cross, living into a community that is known by a peculiar marginality as well as a scandalous promise.

Somehow, despite the superficiality of the church, our memory clings to us still, in part by way of the memory of Scripture. As a background for the display case mentioned earlier is a large poster, showing a road disappearing into a featureless horizon. Over that horizon are the following words from Mark 8:34: "[Jesus] called the crowd with his disciples, and said to them, 'If any want to become my followers, let them deny themselves and take up their cross and follow me.'" The juxtaposition of the empty horizon and Jesus' call to discipleship strikes me as telling: while the future of the captive often appears bleak and without meaning, for the one who follows Jesus the horizon changes by virtue of what we are told to take as well as by the One we are called to follow.

---

3. Quoted in ibid., 36.

Too often, when people speak of their "calling" it bears little resemblance to the stunning, ultimately scandalous invitation we hear in Mark. "I'm called to rural ministry," or "to urban ministry," or "hospital chaplaincy"—these sound all too much like an undergraduate talking about whether she or he will major in biology or psychology, something chosen as a matter of preference, or ability, or, more likely, profitability. It also bears the imprint of the culture of specialists, in which each specific profession claims exclusive forms of knowledge, knowledge inaccessible to those in other professions. My concerns arise not around the appropriate training for specific callings within the church—these are necessary in order to equip servant-leaders for their particular vocations. A good portion of my life has been dedicated to equipping students as effective and faithful communicators of the gospel through preaching. Yet I am concerned that, given our world setting and the peculiar nature of Christ's calling, contemporary notions of calling are becoming theologically and symbolically anemic—and if that is the case, the faith communities that are called out of the larger society are, in turn, nutrient starved.

The horizon of the church becomes banal without the specific character of Christ and cross forming its basic narrative. Perhaps that is why the experience of the refugee seems evocative for our calling to the churches of today. Rather than having a potluck of choices, the called community is confronted by the profoundly disorienting event of the cross, an apocalyptic event that fuels a tectonic shift in the church's way of being. Before the community experiences a specific vocational direction, it resembles the experience of the refugee, reflecting that sense of profound dislocation. Speechlessness, according to Richard Lischer, describes the characteristic state of the prophetic calling:

> Before any prophet speaks, the prophet is absolutely positive that he or she must *not* speak. Moses claimed a speech impediment; Isaiah confessed his own impurity; Jeremiah appealed to his inexperience. After the temple was destroyed, the prophet Ezekiel was transported to a refugee camp at Tel Abib. There he sat for seven days stupefied among the refugees, or, as one translation has it, "in a catatonic state."[4]

The called community is asked to go by a path not of its own choosing—indeed, it is asked to go by a path that it positively would *not*

---

4. Lischer, *The End of Words*, 5–6.

choose—but a path of God's own electing, a path sanctified by the Spirit long before it was ever credentialed by the powers, secular or sacral. If we were to locate our sense of calling in the context or experience of the exilic community, we might well be drawn closer to the experience of Abraham and Sarah, the father and mother of refugees, living as strangers in a strange land—and strangers not only because of their exilic status but also because of the promise of God, a promise that elects alien, stranger, and outcast alike as a new people in an ancient world.

Callings in this sort of community would be startling on the earthly horizon, particularly in a society accustomed to the vacancy of hope and the abundance of fear that frequently define life in exile. Here we would find fewer fantasies about a return to "the way things were" as well as less resignation to the way things are. The former group insists on clinging to a past that is no more, while the latter assimilate, choosing "integration" over resistance. There is no shortage of churches content with either assimilationist resignation or isolationist fantasies: they are some of the fastest-growing churches in North America. By contrast, a faith community with a strong cruciform identity will be peculiar, even activist in its spirit, because it is in the world but not of the world, the promise of God being decisive for its living witness. As Gerhard Forde points out, "The cross itself is the evidence that we did not choose [Christ] but that he, nevertheless, chose us."[5] A church like this and a calling like this will leave some evidence in the earth of its being, some fissure or wound that has become, improbably, a visible demonstration of Spirit and power.

III

A startling image appears in Karl Barth's collection of sermons, *Deliverance to the Captives*. In these sermons preached while he served as a chaplain to prisoners, Barth makes the astounding assertion that the first church consisted of the two criminals who died with Jesus at the crucifixion:

> The promise is given and is valid wherever men [and women] may suffer and die as criminals with Jesus. This promise and nothing else constitutes the Christian community and makes man [or woman] a Christian. These two criminals were the first two who,

---

5. Forde, *On Being a Theologian of the Cross*, 51.

suffering and dying with Jesus, were gathered by this promise into the Christian fold.[6]

Barth admonishes his listeners "'to get in line' behind the two criminals who were first on Golgotha" and were, as such, the first to be "covered by [Christ's] promise."[7] Setting aside questions of their faith, Barth privileges, through God's promise, a disenfranchised community (or a people who were not a nation) as the evangelizing community.

What would happen if we took Barth's sermon to the captives seriously? What would our "callings" look like if we were to "get in line behind" the crucified peoples of the world, peoples covered by the promise most visibly? What would it be like for the church to understand its ministry as existing "outside the gates," existing with refugee and exile, learning to die with this community, covered by Christ's promise? And, then, how would our specific vocation change, knowing that by taking up our cross, we are also being clothed by Christ's promise? If Rome uses the cross to destroy counternarratives and annihilate voice, how does Christ's resurrection subvert the culture-annihilating power of Rome with the compassion-weaving, story-evoking power of the gospel? If that promise is decisive for all who die "covered" by Christ, how might that change our talk about calling?

IV

Jürgen Moltmann begins his book *The Crucified God* with this unequivocal declaration: "The cross is not and cannot be loved. Yet only the crucified Christ can bring the freedom which changes the world because it is no longer afraid of death."[8] As the way of the cross is the way of our calling, we cannot express calling in terms of a professional assortment of options. When the disciples left behind tools and skills, not to mention families, they were not so much abandoning the utility of these skills as they were surrendering every work to the work of the cross, which can never be other than a holy mystery. Before calling is conceived as practical art it must be an act of surrendering works to what Luther calls the "alien" work of God in Christ and his cross. That alien work, according to Forde, is *against* us before it is *for* us: "God does his alien and wrath-

---

6. Barth, *Deliverance to the Captives*, 82.
7. Ibid., 83, 82.
8. Moltmann, *The Crucified God*, 1.

ful work before he does his proper and loving work; he makes alive by killing, brings to heaven by going through hell, brings forth mercy out of wrath."[9]

We perhaps see evidence of God's "againstness" in the disarray left behind in the wake of callings. Many view the decision to leave behind vocations and skills, or at least to set them to one side in pursuit of ministry, as a "sacrifice" indicative of a person's determination to follow God. Without that sacrifice some might question the authenticity or depth of the decision to pursue ministry. We often take the visible signs of a life left behind as testimony that yes, indeed, God claims this person's life in a particular way, rattling the known with the promise of an as-yet undisclosed future.

But what we seem less equipped to articulate is what this means for the formation of communities. That is to say, while we romanticize the leaving of community, there is a dearth of community formation at a popular level. It is almost as if, when speaking of calling, our language has been coopted by the narratives of corporate systems rather than community formation. Like the nineteenth- and twentieth-century missionaries who often ignored, at great cost, the distinction between American conquest and gospel mission, we, too, confuse narratives of displacement with biblical narratives of calling. While today the language of conquest has ebbed, the language of corporate America floods the airwaves, dominating our national and religious identity, imposing its own kind of "calling" where people are routinely displaced or replaced.

According to Peter T. Kilborn's *Next Stop, Reloville: Life Inside America's New Rootless Professional Class*, "Relos" (the name adopted by those who are routinely displaced by the economic patterns of corporate America) "inflate the American Dream and put it on wheels."[10] The lives of the "Relos" follow the dictates and needs of corporate America, as they follow the money trail from one bland suburb to the next, taking along with them "an insular, portable, and parallel culture with little recognized but real implications for American society at large."[11] As it turns out, some of those implications bear directly on the kinds of communities that pastors serve:

---

9. Forde, *On Being a Theologian of the Cross*, 31.
10. Kilborn, *Next Stop, Reloville*, 4.
11. Ibid.

> Like most Americans, Relos value their health, homes, jobs, weekends, and immediate neighbors—at least, that is, while they are among them. They get Christmas cards from the last subdivision, but after a couple of years the cards stop. Relos don't have accents. Wherever they go, they don't belong. Their kids don't know where they are from. Relos don't know where their funerals will be or who might come.... Relos tend to know mostly other Relos, from their offices, subdivisions, PTAs, and kids soccer and baseball teams. *At Reloville megachurches . . . none of the parishioners acknowledged me. Then I noticed that no one acknowledged anyone.*[12]

Wendell Berry offers a more trenchant assessment of our current economic system for our reflection:

> Most people are now finding that they are free to make very few significant choices. It is becoming steadily harder for ordinary people—the unrich, the unprivileged—to choose a kind of work for which they have a preference, a talent, or a vocation, to choose where they will live . . . or even to choose to raise their own children. . . . And most individuals ("liberated" or not) choose to conform not to local ways and conditions but to a rootless and placeless monoculture of commercial expectations and products. . . . We want the liberty of divorce from spouses and independence from family and friends, yet we remain indissolubly married to a hundred corporations that regard us at best as captives and at worst as prey.[13]

As I read those words, I began to squirm my way into reflection, self-examination: "How am I any different, really?"

I added up the places I have lived for a grand total of ten different cities (and I cannot count how many different apartments and houses) in my lifetime, ranging from as far north as Alaska, where I was born, to as far south as South Carolina (my first ministerial call), living in most of those places for just a few years. From the beginning of graduate school to the present, spanning roughly twenty years, I have lived in five different cities, reaching from coast to coast. At present, I live in a city where I have no extended family and a place I would not call "home." Yet, when someone asks, "Where is home for you?" I am at a loss. But the problem is not mine only; it extends to my daughters, too. I am not comfortable saying Iowa is their home, even though they were born here. The resemblances layer one

---

12. Ibid., 5 (Italics mine).
13. Berry, *Sex, Economy, Freedom, and Community*, 151–52.

on top of the other. "Still," I say to myself, "I am different . . . or at least, I would like to be different." More broadly, we might ask ourselves, "How are we different, how do callings to the ministry of the church or simply being active in a church alter our relationship to the rootless landscape we have inherited from corporate America?"

One has to wonder if the theological content of calling has experienced some slippage, giving way to a culture created by conquest and commercial ambition, where location is viewed as transient and unimportant, and corporate headquarters (read "high steeple"), wherever it may be, is all that matters. Apart from the inherent absenteeism implied by transiency, no real community can be formed in a "call" that lasts just three years.[14] But the reverse is also true: pastoral identity will not receive much in the way of what congregations have to offer in terms of formation. As it is, our contemporary understandings and practice of call create disarray, for the pastor and his or her family as well as the church. And the witness of the church? Far from being countercultural, our callings are neither deep nor lasting.

At some point we need to ask ourselves the question, To what extent are we answering the "call" of a financial system, participating in the mindlessness of a new era of financial colonialism? And if that is the case, what are we in danger of losing? What have we lost? And just as importantly, how might we begin to recover a sense of place while also honoring the narrative of calling?

Some might object to this concern, claiming I am making "much ado about nothing," particularly pointing to Jesus' itinerancy and that well-known itinerant, Paul, as expressions of calling that should not be ignored. None of these servants of the church "remained" in a place, but were constantly on the move, their stories peppered with myriad place names and peoples. Seen this way, disciples look rather more like polished consultants than people very much acquainted with communion. Still, popular symbols of missionary activity seem to corroborate this reading. Who, for example, is not familiar with the Bible maps showing Paul's travels throughout the Mediterranean world? Or what about sitting through, as I did growing up, the flickering slide shows of missionaries who worked with the poor? The slides usually showed people of color (the

---

14. I am not speaking of intentional interim ministry, which plays an important role in congregational transitions, but, rather, the shortness of pastoral tenures as well as the high numbers of pastors who drop out of the ministry after only a few years of service.

poor) standing next to their white benefactor (the wealthy). The presenter would talk, and then, as he proceeded to the next slide, we were returned to our momentary darkness, but never for too long, lest we lose the message that we were as light to those in darkness. These pictures created a propaganda of transiency, promoting not the significance of place or person but only passing through places. It seems self-evident that transience most aptly describes calling, always on the move, constantly changing places, and trading communities with an "amen" and benediction thrown in for pious measure.

But we know different. Though Jesus was constantly on the move he was even more constant in the formation of distinctly counterintuitive expressions of the reign of God: feasting with "tax collectors and sinners"; talking alone with a Syro-Phoenician woman; being touched by and touching the unclean; receiving the tears and praise of prostitutes who knew themselves as his sisters and daughters. Everywhere we witness Jesus forming community where before there was only blank-faced displacement. What we see in the Gospel accounts show that Jesus is not a transient figure but a figure who turns the transient characters of the world into lasting testimonies of God's salvific work. Around each testimony, one hears the words, to borrow from Brian Blount's expression, "Go tell! Go preach!"[15]—words that beget communities and nations where neither existed before.

Another "transient" figure, Paul, in particular expresses lasting pastoral affection for each of the communities to which he was connected. Each and every one of his letters, even his most ferocious of letters, Galatians, begins with thanksgiving. And when we remember his name, we remember place names: Romans, Galatians, Philippi, Thessalonica, and so on. Paul's attachment to these places? He cannot express it; ordinary language collapses on his otherwise capable tongue. Language and anthropology collide and collapse, as he portrays his affection, even his own body, in the shocking metaphor of a nursing mother, his longing like that of an orphan yearning for its mother, or a woman in the pain of childbirth "until Christ is formed in you" (Gal. 4:19).[16] Paul's employment of such startlingly transgressive imagery suggests that we might be mistaken to merely call it "mutual love" though that was probably present,

---

15. Blount, *Go Preach! Mark's Kingdom Message and the Black Church Today*.
16. See Gaventa, *Our Mother Saint Paul*, 25–8.

at least in some circumstances. Mutual love, after all, implies reciprocity, but Paul employs asymmetrical language, completely destabilizing the edifice of reciprocity with something else and something other, defying conventional tropes with the unconventional metaphor.

Paul uses provocative imagery, according to Beverly Roberts Gaventa, because of his identification with the crucified Jesus. Explaining Paul's description of himself as a nursing mother in 1 Corinthians 3:1–2, Gaventa writes, ". . . the images of apostolic ministry Paul employs in chapter 3 have their origin in his proclamation of the crucified Jesus, who is no more a 'real man' by the world's standards than is a nursing Paul."[17] Because he proclaims Christ and him crucified, the One who takes his place among the cursed, among the misshapen, and the disfigured, or the transgendered, Paul discovers and proclaims community where only alienation and condemnation was known before. And he did so after the manner of Jesus, who took his peculiar place in the cosmos, digging into the desolate landscape of Golgotha, where the economic and religious trends were clearly not in his favor but the promise was at least as pronounced as his most self-evident love.

If we return to the call narratives of the disciples in the Gospels, what we see, in fact, are narrations of calling to inhabit true community, shattering economic pretense with Real Presence.

V

According to Barth, the captives were "covered" by the promise. Despite all appearances, they were clothed with the promise. That language should incite us to insinuate a basic economic and cultural endeavor into our narratives of calling—we must be about the business of forming leaders and communities who are committed to the vocation of clothing the refugee in the many-patterned traditions of culture and economy. If calling involves leaving behind, it also involves weaving together a new fabric, distinctive to place and people and story. What I mean here finds its best evocation in the first report of exilic experience, after Adam and Eve were driven "east of Eden." God appears again, joining the exiles whom God has exiled, but this time God's mercy eclipses God's judgment with the richly suggestive image of the intimate tenderness of the Creator knitting together animal skins, as shelter and comfort for the refugee, an act of

17. Ibid., 50.

mercy as well as an act of the indigenous economy, drawing from the creation sacred cloth for joyful, full-bodied living.

Sally Brown believes that cruciform preaching engages in both critical and constructive homiletical work.[18] Extending this language in a more metaphorical direction, on the one hand, I would say the work of preaching good news involves crafting new clothing for the community, grafting God's story to our stories. Perhaps this could be understood as a basic impulse at work in Christ who, though being equal with God, takes human form, becoming obedient as a slave, even to the point of dying on a cross. The witness of the cross offers a "critical" witness to the church. On the other hand, the sermon participates in the delicate work of clothing the crucified and the exiled, weaving together the textiles of words and metaphor, materials that come from our life here on earth, even as we witness to our citizenship in heaven. Such materials will reflect courageous, confident, and joyful living into contemporary social and political realities.

But before we are clothed with the song of redemption, we were "clothed" with the straitjacket of death. In John's account of the raising of Lazarus, he comes out of the tomb, still captive to death. John actually says more than this—according to John he was still dead, even as he walked out of the tomb: "The dead man came out, his hands and feet bound with strips of cloth, and his face wrapped in a cloth. Jesus said to them, 'Unbind him, and let him go'" (John 11:44). As preachers and church communities participate in this freedom, together we "unbind" the false claims of death, and begin the process of clothing our refugee identity with the skins of grace and mercy, drawn from the creation, out of the dusts of displacement, joining Christ's liberation of the dead into the resurrection song of God's kingdom community.

---

18. Brown, *Cross Talk: Preaching Redemption*, 63.

1

People of the Penguin

IF PREACHING IN AN academic community revels in the articulation of the theological tradition writ large, preaching in the local community of faith reminds us that the sermon is bathed in the particular histories, symbols, stories, heartbreaks, and hopes of local communities. One could say this kind of preaching anchors the historical tradition of the church. Without the local church and its preachers engaging in local theology, our theological traditions may lack the contextual ballast that keeps the tradition on an even keel.

In her book, *Preaching as Local Theology and Folk Art*, Nora Tisdale makes the following observation: "The preacher is . . . a 'folk artist'— searching for the expression of local theology through symbols, forms, and movements that are capable of capturing and transforming the imaginations of a particular local community of faith."[1] Given the sense that seminary preaching finds its original font in the intricacies of local communities of faith, it is perhaps fitting that the first sermon of this collection should be from a congregation, in this instance an Alaska Native community, in Metlakatla, Alaska.

My relationship to this congregation was, as with most of my congregational preaching, that of a supply pastor. Within this setting, however, my relationship to the community was layered with historical as well as ethnic dimensions, since my ancestry is Athabascan and German. While I can "pass" as an ordinary white American, I was preceded by two generations of Native people who were persecuted for their ethnicity, struggling to survive in a culture that was hostile to their skins as well as

---

1. Tisdale, *Preaching as Local Theology and Folk Art*, 124.

their stories. Indeed, part of the reason I can "pass" today can be assigned to policies of assimilation. Some Native people with "mixed ancestry" describe themselves as "genetically engineered," underscoring the political and economic forces of assimilation. But assimilation also extended to religion so that when Native people became Christian, it was as if they turned in their Native identity. In the view of the larger public, Native Christian people, whether they were of mixed ancestry or pure blood, lost their skins. It is in this context that telling our stories as Native peoples, or people of mixed ancestry, is a critical act as well as constructive one, returning us to our skins, clothing us with the narratives of our ancestors, with the regalia of village and tribe.

Preaching can be seen, I suppose, as offering clothing for the church, and yet, the first missionaries were determined to strip Native people of their ancestral story. Our ancestors were told, in so many words, that the skins of the tribe (language, geographies, rites, arts, myths) were anti-Christian or, at best, not Christian enough. Whereas much of America's "folk art" might find acceptance in the church's worship, Native expressions and identities are not so welcomed. Historically, pastors to Native congregations often took a dim view of things Native. More contemporaneously, without understanding Native people or our histories, pastors rode roughshod over the actual meanings of cultural practices, disregarding Native concerns in a high-handed "liberation" that created more problems than solutions. This makes the work of local theology especially complex for Native churches and their pastors in North America.

It was in this context that Mark's Gospel, which came from the Lord's Day readings in the Revised Common Lectionary, spoke to me, and especially to the people of the Metlakatla Presbyterian Church, a Tsimshian village with a well-known missionary history. As with many Native Christian peoples, there is a sense of acute "out-of-placeness" or "scandal" in claiming a dual identity, as Barbara Fawcett (Tlingit) pointedly expressed, as she showed me her collection of baskets and masks, declaring, "I am Native *and* Christian!"

It struck me that Mark's Gospel witnesses to startling and even scandalous scenarios of displacement and identity: a demoniac rushing, pell-mell, into the synagogue; an unclean woman touching the hem of Jesus' robe; the Gerasene demoniac raging among the tombs, raging against chains of so-called civilization; the Syro-Phoenician woman, viewed by the "insiders" as an unclean "outsider," and yet who, alone in the Gospel of Mark, seems to "win" in the question-and-answer game with the Son of God. Mark's Gospel seems to revel in Jesus' willingness to dance with people who have lost the art of dance, who seem out of place in the kingdom of God. But through the Gospel, the lame dance and the mute sing for joy.

As I mentioned above, one of the images of God that I find especially evocative for the work of preaching is that of God-as-Seamstress: "And the Lord God made garments of skins for the man and for his wife, and clothed them" (Gen. 3:21). This image is found elsewhere as well, in Mark 5:15 ("They came to Jesus and saw the demoniac sitting there, clothed and in his right mind, the very man who had had the legion; and they were afraid"), in Colossians 3:12 (". . . clothe yourselves with compassion, kindness, humility, meekness, and patience"), as well as in allusions to baptismal garments (e.g., Mark 16:5; Gal. 3:27). At heart, however, the core story is that of a God who grafts God's own skin to open wounds, grafting divine life to naked humanity. As preachers who tell stories of and for congregations and peoples, some of whom have been stripped naked by injustices, skin lashed with prejudice, and spirits crushed by the smug arrogance of those who possess power, the sermon can become a most delicate expression of God's compassion in a crushing world. The sermon below reflects, I hope, this sense of vocation, clothing the human being with skins of companionship, memory, dignity, and hope.

THE PEOPLE OF THE PENGUIN[2]

And [Jesus] said to [the disciples], "How many loaves have you? Go and see." When they had found out, they said, "Five, and two fish." Then he ordered them to get all the people to sit down in groups on the green grass. So they sat down in groups of hundreds and of fifties. Taking the five loaves and the two fish, he looked up to heaven, and blessed and broke the loaves, and gave them to his disciples to set before the people; and he divided the two fish among them all. And all ate and were filled; and they took up twelve baskets full of broken pieces and of the fish. Those who had eaten the loaves numbered five thousand men. (Mark 6:38-44)

---

2. The sermon title plays on the four clans that make up Tsimshian community (Raven, Eagle, Wolf, and Killer Whale). As I reflected on the experience of being "out of place," I chose this well-known bird to inaugurate a "fifth" imaginary clan, notable primarily for its awkwardness.

After calling the different clans to the Invitational Dance, the leader of the dance, David Boxley Jr., invited those of us who were, as he put it, "people without a clan" to join them on the Long House dance floor. At first, we were hesitant, reluctant to risk being out of place. But soon, overcoming fear, we, too, joined the circle of dancers, moving to the beat and call of traditional Tsimshian chants and drums.[3]

Before too long, we were gliding through the sky, tilting our imaginary wings like Eagles resting on a gentle breeze; or we were undulating through the ocean depths like the Killer Whale; or running like the Wolf; or calling like the Raven. Or so we thought. In truth, there was probably more hospitality on that floor than skilled dancers. To put it less charitably, we flattered ourselves in thinking that we were dancing the dances of the different clans—the dancers of the clans danced in the tradition of their elders, a tradition passed down from generation to generation for tens of thousands of years. We, however, were rather new to the Tsimshian dance floor—whatever we were dancing it did not quite fit in any one of the clan dances. Perhaps some might have said there were a few penguins mixing with the communities of the Killer Whale, Raven, Eagle, and Wolf. Some might have even said there was a "fifth" clan—the Penguin clan—dancing among the other four.

Why a "penguin"? Strange sort of animal to choose for a clan, don't you think? Not very noble, not noted for its graceful movement. Known mostly for its awkward out-of-placeness. And maybe that's it . . . maybe that is why a penguin is a good symbol for an imaginary "fifth clan"—that is, even though the penguin has wings, it cannot soar like the Eagle—perhaps a little angry beating of wind, a squawk, a thumping of webbed feet on cold ice—but no soaring, not for the penguin. Maybe the penguin would run like the wolf, but he can barely manage a waddle. A penguin has the colors of the Killer Whale, but he is neither a killer nor a whale. And when God was handing out brains, the Raven, always a bit of an opportunist, was first in line . . . the penguin, just like always, got the leftovers.

***

---

3. Although I am Native (Athabascan), in some traditionalist circles I am viewed as an outsider, especially since I am a relative novice in the cultural renewal movement that began in earnest in the last decade or so.

People of the Penguin

The penguin: an odd sort of creature, neither one nor the other, fitting for the unfit. It may be that the Penguin clan is a good clan for those folks who feel like a square peg in a round world, who feel left out in an in-crowd, for those who are lost in a world of the found, for those who would soar but can only beat at the wind, for those who've lost their cunning and for those who never had it, for Ravens who are weary of winning, for Killer Whales who have lost their courage, for those who feel like misfits in a world of the fashionably fit—maybe the Penguin clan is a good clan for those folks who are a little out of place on the dance floor of the world.

In a way, you could say that Mark is a story about the People of the Penguin, or the beginnings of the church. That is to say, the people who surrounded Jesus in this Gospel got the short end of the stick in almost every way. They were the mentally insane and the demon possessed, they were those afflicted by chronic disease of both body and mind, they were the thirsty whose thirst could not be quenched, they were the hungry for whom no ordinary bread was satisfying, they were the hopeless in desperate search of hope, they were the cold in a world without warmth, they were those who could not adjust to a maladjusted world—they were, in short, a People of the Penguin, a people who were all but left behind. . . .

Left behind except for Jesus. This Jesus wades into the worlds of the Penguin. Jesus himself, Jesus fully God and fully human, wades into the worlds of the oppressed and the dispossessed. He wades into crowds of misfits and toothless grins, he wades into what others have called "disposable people"—and he gathers them, each one, the broken pieces that everyone else left behind.

∗∗∗

But I have a confession to make, a confession just between us Penguins: I don't have a lot of love for my fellow Penguins. I'm not like Jesus. I don't understand why he bothers with these welfare people, why he bothers with their broken hearts and shattered dreams, don't understand why he troubles himself with their lost causes. I can't explain why he cares so deeply when his care will go unrewarded, unacknowledged, unappreciated. Like other Penguins, I don't want to be a Penguin . . . and I don't want their company either.

I was a pastor, a long way from here, living in South Carolina. I wanted to get away from the penguin people. You'd be surprised how many Penguins live in South Carolina. My mother was coming out to visit. So we went to Edisto Island—a place where Penguins are few and far between—or so I imagined.

Once we got there we started walking on the beach, beach combing, looking for shells. There were plenty to choose from: seashells, more than you could imagine, occasionally a shark tooth, more often a sand dollar, but mostly they were the kinds of shells you would pass by as you searched for something better—that is, unless you were my mother.

We'd not been walking for too long, I'd found two or three good conch shells—no cracks, clean-looking things, the inside the soft color of pearl and the outside pink like the color of freshness itself—it was about that time that I noticed my mother: her arms were overflowing with shells, most if not all of them broken. She had so many she'd taken off her coat and made it into a bag to hold them all and even that was not enough. I asked her why she was picking up all the broken ones, and, handing me a shell to carry, she said, "The broken ones are the most beautiful."

***

"And all ate and were filled; and they took up twelve baskets full of broken pieces and of the fish" (42–3).

After that lovely meal, with those five thousand fed and fully satisfied, you would think that the story would have went something like this: "And after they were all completely satisfied, they took a nice nap, there on the grass in the cooling evening, some talking, some just resting, some quiet and reflective." If you or I had written the story, it might have gone something like that.

But something different happens in this story. After all the people were satisfied, the disciples went out and began gathering up the broken piece of bread and fish, twelve baskets full. The writer is not telling us that Jesus was simply a little overly exuberant in his miracle making. Instead, the writer is telling us that Jesus was in the business of nation building—of a kind quite different from the kind of nation building that is in vogue these days. Those twelve baskets represent the twelve tribes of Israel, the covenant nation of God. But instead of being filled with beautiful, perfect people, those baskets, those tribes were filled with broken people, people with broken hearts and broken minds, people with toothless grins and problems with depression, people who drank too much, and people who wept too much, people who could not forget, and people who could not forgive.

They were the People of the Penguin.

One might imagine all those Penguin People in one place letting out a groan so complete in its misery that not even heaven could bear it. That such a people would erupt in a surge of misery and frustration, a gong of failure, an unending cry of sadness. But in this story, like before, it is different.

Like the crowds that gathered around Jesus in the Gospel of Mark,

> we, too, have come to this dance floor—

> perhaps when we came we felt the risk too risky, the awkwardness too deep—after all, we were Eagles who were afraid to fly;

Killer Whales who had lost their courage;

> Wolves who could only whimper;

> and Ravens whose genius had lost its luster.

But on the dance floor of God's purpose, we are joined with the drums of doxology and the chants of faith—we find in here, in this place, a new song in our hearts, a new dance being born within use, a dance where no one is a stranger but each one of us belongs.

Whoever you may be, from whatever corner of this blue planet you have come,

> > you are invited to this dance.

> All the clans of the world are gathered here . . .

> > and we are dancing,

> like the Eagles dance,

> > like the Killer Whale,

> the Wolf

> > and the Raven—

> all of us, the People of the Penguin,

dancing to the drumbeat of doxology. Amen.

The Metlakatla Presbyterian Church
Metlakatla, Alaska
July 20, 2003

2

Travel Advisories

Most who experience seminary chapel on a regular basis will recognize a message that appears in various forms throughout the year, the "our-experience-of-seminary-is-forty-years-of-wandering" sermon. As a student I was more sympathetic with these sermons than I am now as a faculty member. Perhaps I am just getting older, crankier, and more critical of those who use the chapel pulpit as a convenient opportunity for pious grumbling. At the same time, having heard that sermon a number of times, arguing against it seems too cranky, even for me. Seminary presents students with enormous challenges, ranging from experiences of leaving house and home, neglecting family and friends, and the like. After a while, maybe seminary feels a bit like a wilderness, an unhappy place. Obviously, other places count as "wilderness" experiences, a diagnosis with cancer or the experience of divorce, for example. But because the place we call wilderness is also seminary it takes on a different valence in our memory. The particular nature of the seminary journey emerged for me as I reflected on Luke's account of Jesus' calling the disciples to "take nothing" with them as they began their journey.

Not surprisingly, seminarians are perhaps especially sensitive to the question of call. That question never leaves us, but I think it is true that seminarians come to this question feeling as though a lot is riding on how they answer that call, whether they are equipped to answer that call, whether they are really called, and so forth. For that reason, a seminary community may hear Jesus' imperative, "take nothing with you," with considerable anxiety. When contemplating a challenging journey, we would like to be prepared, and that is what seminary is about or at least we hope that is what it is about.

Of course, as you will see, it was not so much our goals in terms of seminary curriculum or spiritual formation that opened this text for me, as it was Rebecca, my spouse and the mother of our two daughters, who shared with me her own sense of vocation as she prepared for one of the most harrowing experiences I have ever witnessed: childbirth.

As I think about it, maybe it was fitting that a woman supplied the interpretive key to unlock this text in Luke's Gospel. After all, the writer of Luke seems peculiarly interested in telling not only the story of Jesus' conception, as does Matthew, but also Mary's experience of carrying the life of God in her womb—an experience at once harrowing and holy— and perhaps not entirely unlike answering a call to ministry.

TRAVEL ADVISORIES

Then Jesus called the twelve together and gave them power and authority over all demons and to cure diseases, and he sent them out to proclaim the kingdom of God and to heal. He said to them, "Take nothing for your journey, no staff, nor bag, nor bread, nor money—not even an extra tunic. Whatever house you enter, stay there, and leave from there. Wherever they do not welcome you, as you are leaving that town shake the dust off your feet as a testimony against them." They departed and went through the villages, bringing the good news and curing diseases everywhere.

Now Herod the ruler heard about all that had taken place, and he was perplexed, because it was said by some that John had been raised from the dead, by some that Elijah had appeared, and by others that one of the ancient prophets had arisen. Herod said, "John I beheaded; but who is this about whom I hear such things?" And he tried to see him.

On their return the apostles told Jesus all they had done. He took them with him and withdrew privately to a city called Bethsaida. When the crowds found out about it, they followed him; and he welcomed them, and spoke to them about the kingdom of God, and healed those who needed to be cured.

The day was drawing to a close, and the twelve came to him and said, "Send the crowd away, so that they may go into the surrounding villages and countryside, to lodge and get provisions; for we are here in a deserted place." But he said to them, "You give them something to eat." They said, "We have no more than five loaves and two fish—unless we are to go and buy food for all these people." For there were about five thousand men. And he said to his disciples, "Make them sit down in groups of about fifty each." They did so and made them all sit down. And taking the five loaves and the two fish, he looked up to heaven, and blessed and broke them, and gave them to the disciples to set before the crowd. And all ate and were filled. What was left over was gathered up, twelve baskets of broken pieces. (Luke 9:1–17)

We are accustomed to travel advisories these days, with their ominous suggestions of criminal intent hidden in the innocent guise of water bottles, gels, razors, and the like. As we walk through the metal detector in the airport, we might well find a sign reading, "Surrender everything, all ye who enter here." There is probably a small fortune of confiscated gels gathering in airports across the country. And, of course, not surprisingly, there has been some complaining of late, objections to the severity of the ban on what we can take along with us for the ride.

With this at the back of our minds, having heard Jesus' travel advisories in Luke, we may thank God that Jesus is *just* our Savior and not the director of the Federal Aviation Authority. If Luke is any indication, Jesus' travel advisories are enormously impractical:

Take nothing for your journey.

No staff, nor bag, nor bread, nor money, not even an extra tunic.

Between you and me, I have a sneaking suspicion that Jesus' advisory might also include such things as that extra pair of clean underwear that I've been taking along with me ever since my mother told me it was a good idea to do so.

We might wonder, "What's Jesus got against that extra tunic, never mind a clean pair of underwear? Wasn't he listening to Mom?" We might start there, but it might be more helpful to focus instead on the verbs in this text:

Jesus *gathers* the twelve,

    Jesus *empowers* the twelve,

        Jesus *sends* the twelve to proclaim the kingdom of God.

Gathering, empowering, and sending: it sounds suspiciously missional, perhaps even the beginning of the missionary church itself.

In fact, many interpreters read this text as a sort of commissioning, a commission that contains three different themes for the missional life of the church. One theme focuses on the hospitality that should be characteristic of the church's missionary life. In other words, Jesus is saying, "Go to the place where I send you, eat the food they eat, speak the language they speak, dress in the clothing in which they dress (don't bring along your special dietary needs, your lactose intolerance, your official languages, and the rest). Go there, rather, in the spirit of hospitality, go there in the spirit that I have come to you, even as open as an infant to the face of the mother."

Another interpretation focuses on the adopted poverty of the missional church. Paraphrasing Bernard of Clairvaux, the disciple of Jesus does not preach the gospel for his or her daily bread, but takes daily bread in order to preach the gospel. The proclamation of the gospel will not be held hostage to those who give bread, but only to the One who is himself bread for the world.

The final interpretation of Luke's travel advisory is the one that I want to explore with you this morning: this advisory is not so much about what we shall or shall not take, but a reminder to the missional church of its total dependence on God. In other words, Jesus is saying,

> Take nothing,

> because where you are going, only I can send you;

> take nothing,

> because when you are sent by me,

>> you go not by the light of your understanding,

>> but by the darkness of my mystery. . . .

> When you are sent by me,

>> take your maps if you must,

> read your ten thousand pages of Barth,

>> master your declensions,

> become a homiletical artiste,

>> but whatever you take,

Remember that what you take pales in comparison to the One who has gathered you, empowered you, and sent you in his name.

So it is more about the *who* than the *what*. But there might be something else as well. Specifically this: to take nothing into the world is, in effect, to die to the world's imperatives, its demands, and even its powers.

In his collection of essays, *The Unforeseen Wilderness*, Wendell Berry writes that by comparison to the usual way of travel, ordinarily supported by countless machines, highways, restaurants, and motels, "the [person] who walks into the wilderness is naked indeed. He leaves behind his work, his household, his duties, his comforts—even, if he comes alone, his words. He immerses himself in what he is not. It is a kind of death."[1]

Not so very long ago, many of you gathered in this chapel, each one surrendering something that was precious, something that had given ballast and hope in another day: some left family in faraway places in very uncertain circumstances; others left everything familiar, from the smell of food to the feel of the air itself; some left professions at which they had worked hard for most of their adult lives; others left beloved pets, homes, friends. While what was left behind was as varied as the worlds we call home, each left a past for a future that could not be fully known, a wilderness which we could not quite imagine.

Indeed, it is a kind of death, not to know.

Jason, a longtime colleague and friend, often refers to seminary as the "cemetery"—now that I am teaching in one, he never fails to make his little joke, to his apparent amusement. To be honest, I find his humor somewhat too predictable, but he is at least partly correct: there is something dying here, something of our inherited world, something even of our seriousness about things which in the presence of Jesus and his kingdom seem more silly than serious.

Believe it or not, I've learned something about how serious things can be rendered silly in the last week or so. As I said earlier, Rebecca and I made a journey last week that we had been anticipating for a little over nine months. As we drew closer to the glorious month of October, our home was the scene of some very serious, even necessary preparations: the spare room was turned into a nursery; Gwendoline, our two-year-old, was graduated from a crib to a bed; and the basement was turned into a spare room to accommodate the grandparents.

> Then, near the close of the day,
>
> perhaps less than a week before the glorious day

---

1. Berry, *The Unforeseen Wilderness*, 57.

of Imogen's imminent arrival,

a day that had gone from *preparing* for her arrival,

to *counting* the interval of minutes between contractions,

at the end of one such day,

>Rebecca said

>>she had to do one more thing,

maybe even an unnecessary thing before she went into labor:

she said she had to paint her toenails . . .

>she couldn't go into labor without her toenails

painted, and that no less in a lovely, dark,

>indulgent red.

It was silly, she said, not because it was primarily frivolous, but because she knew that by comparison to the labor pains that bring forth life, it was as if it were naught.

>Even more, by comparison

>>to little Imogen's first yawp of life,

>by comparison to the feeling of holding,

>>of seeing, of being gathered face to face,

>>of skin to skin,

>>of eye seeing eye,

>>of hands holding hands—

by comparison to all that, Rebecca knew that her toenail needs were less than nothing, and maybe they were just silly.

Maybe so. But somehow, I just can't see Jesus begrudging an expectant mother's toenail needs. Maybe he would say that such a thing was silly, but maybe he would say it was silly in a necessary sort of way.

Consider, for instance, the text we have before us. It seems that Jesus was inviting the disciples to a special kind of folly. It was, after all, Jesus who told them to bring nothing for their journey *and* to feed the five thousand with a few loaves of bread and a couple of fish.

It was silliness to take what was indulgent perhaps for a few, a blessing for the twelve, daily bread for the believers, and offer it to the five thousand—an offering that could only be silly by comparison to the hungers of the thousands.

The disciples, hearing what Jesus would have them do, are predictably appalled. That is, like many of us, they are tempted to be all too serious about their bread and fish, perhaps even more serious about these than they are about Jesus the Christ, the One who gathered them, empowered them, and sent them.

Perhaps what the disciples forgot then, and what we too easily forget today, is this: it is Jesus who is the folly of God and the power of our salvation. It is Jesus who multiplies the bread and fish, not us; it is Jesus who blesses and gathers a people we would prefer to send away; it is Jesus who dies to this world and its crucifixion imperatives, so that we might be born again, children of the kingdom.

A few loaves of bread, and two fish for five thousand. Perhaps it was silly, after all . . . silly in a necessary, maybe even glorious sort of way.

It is midsemester now. Things are getting serious, in case you haven't noticed. The frivolity of summer is no more. The leaves have turned from green to yellow to red. Even the things that were collected into the Severance Hall display case, just outside the dean's office, the things that memorialized your before-seminary world, the things you gave to symbolize what you were leaving behind, have been taken away, though surely not forgotten, no more forgotten than the fishing nets the disciples left when they answered Jesus' call.[2]

Even so, they are something like the fallen leaves of yesterday's summer, unhinged from their moors, blowing into a future they do not know, a kingdom about which we have only "hints and guesses" . . .[3]

But it might be that these days the hints and guesses about the kingdom are growing . . .

Perhaps we have gone from getting things ready to counting the contractions, and they are growing stronger, more and more serious, more and more difficult to avoid, and perhaps they are growing in you: perhaps the promise of the kingdom is riding lower down in the womb of the church than it has ever been before, the time is full, the kingdom of God

---

2. Each year, as a part of the orientation week, students are invited to bring something symbolizing their lives before coming to seminary, something they left behind to come to seminary. These items are then placed in a display case at one of the main entrances to Severance Hall.

3. Eliot, "The Dry Salvages," in *Four Quartets*, 44.

is near, pressing against the lid of the creation, warning us of our end, our beginning, about to burst into the world.

You may greet these growing contractions of the kingdom as a mixed blessing. Of course, we look forward to the good things of God. It is right to do so. That is why we pray and we sing, because we anticipate the promise of the kingdom. But it is also a little scary to welcome Christ into the world, for he brings a future that we cannot guess, a way we have not known, a world we have only faintly imagined.

And so I say to you today, go on, whether it is necessary or not, pack your bag, paint your toenails, master your declensions, deepen your knowledge, get ready.

Gather a little bread and fish for the journey, even if it seems a bit silly . . . after all, you never know, it just might be a necessary sort of silliness, even to the surpassing glory of God. Amen.

October 18, 2006

3

Mercy on Thin Ice

AMONG THE BENEFITS OF being attached to a university, rather than being a freestanding seminary, is that we are connected to the larger life of contemporary culture, and that closeness is sometimes expressed through shared worship. It was a service of shared worship that led to the sermon below, which was given during a symposium on the role of character formation in higher education. Amid one corporate scandal after another, U.S.-government-sponsored torture, and other disturbing incidents, the University of Dubuque adopted a commitment to character formation within our curriculum. Unlike the other sermons in this collection, the following message had as its principal audience a group of faculty from the university as well as undergraduate students and other guests.

It would be a mistake, however, to imagine that the seminary community and the church it serves were "excused" from attendance. The problem of character is not isolated to the so-called secular world—from seminary presidents to youth pastors, the failure of character education within the church is glaring. While I would like to say it is not the case, the evidence suggests that the seminary has much to learn about character education and this sermon, for its part, was an attempt to participate in that important conversation.

A word or two about the sermon itself may be helpful. When I was asked to preach for the chapel that began our daylong symposium, I fully expected, given my experience, that the lectionary would fail me and I would need to hunt down a text that held promise for the particular question of character formation in higher education. So it was that I was surprised and a little concerned when I saw the lectionary text for that day, Luke's parable of the Good Samaritan. Against the hypothesis that the lectionary would not be apt, it was, in fact, surprisingly apt. But why would I be concerned? Why not be relieved for not having to look for another text? I suppose I was concerned because I am often intimidated by such well-worn texts; in truth, I prefer a text that is a little less frequented by pulpit and pew. Perhaps it is because I believe, rightly or wrongly, that I don't have as much to live up to if the text is unfamiliar.

Apart from the church's familiarity with this text there are problems related to how interpreters typically handle the relationship between people who are "helpers" and those who receive "help." Native readers remind the majority culture that the church has appropriated this text uncritically, turning the Samaritan into a cipher for the majority culture's socioeconomic and racial class. Mission becomes nothing more than a "helping class" (majority-culture, middle-class whites) providing welfare to a needy class (minority-culture nonwhites or the white poor):

> What we are saying . . . is that people need to take a new look at the story of the good [sic] Samaritan. You will recall that a man traveling the Jericho Road was robbed and beaten. Several socially acceptable people passed him in need. It was a Samaritan who stopped to help. The problem, however, is that most people identify themselves as the helper. The Samaritan, however, was despised in his time. He was a contemporary counterpart of the outcast, the disadvantaged, the Nigger, the Brown Beret, and the savage.[1]

This insight upsets the convenient polarities that divide the so-called helping class from the class that often receives help. But it may not go far enough.

While this interpretation rightly advances the unique interpretive location of socially marginalized peoples by reminding us of the sociopolitical character of the Samaritan, we risk losing the more fundamental and ultimately more scandalous narrative of God in Christ. That is, in the end, we do not *proclaim* the *Good Samaritan*, but instead we proclaim the *Wayward Christ*. Using more familiar language, we proclaim Christ crucified, seeing Christ as he joins himself to the despised, the outcast, and the exiled. While Christ is never reducible to any human condition, it is difficult to argue that when Christ appears, his appearing inverts centristic notions of power, place, and person with the scandal of the cross.

1. "We May Be Brothers After All" by the American Indian Consulting Panel, 29–30.

Perhaps that is why, in the end, I try to move the sermon full circle, having the listener first "see" the one who needs help ("the wrong kind of person, in the wrong place, at the wrong time") to identifying himself or herself as that "wrong kind of person" in the world.

MERCY ON THIN ICE

Just then a lawyer stood up to test Jesus. "Teacher," he said, "what must I do to inherit eternal life?" He said to him, "What is written in the law? What do you read there?" He answered, "You shall love the Lord your God with all your heart, and with all your soul, and with all your strength, and with all your mind; and your neighbor as yourself." And he said to him, "You have given the right answer; do this, and you will live."

But wanting to justify himself, he asked Jesus, "And who is my neighbor?" Jesus replied, "A man was going down from Jerusalem to Jericho, and fell into the hands of robbers, who stripped him, beat him, and went away, leaving him half dead. Now by chance a priest was going down that road; and when he saw him, he passed by on the other side. So likewise a Levite, when he came to the place and saw him, passed by on the other side. But a Samaritan while traveling came near him; and when he saw him, he was moved with pity. He went to him and bandaged his wounds, having poured oil and wine on them. Then he put him on his own animal, brought him to an inn, and took care of him. The next day he took out two denarii, gave them to the innkeeper, and said, 'Take care of him; and when I come back, I will repay you whatever more you spend.' Which of these three, do you think, was a neighbor to the man who fell into the hands of the robbers?" He said, "The one who showed him mercy." Jesus said to him, "Go and do likewise." (Luke 10:25–37)

A few years back, *The New York Times* ran a story with the headline, "Through the Cracks, Then Through the Ice." It was about a man who drowned, his body discovered some time after he fell through the ice on Prospect Lake in Brooklyn. But the real story took place long before this man had fallen through the ice of Prospect Lake. Before this, he had fallen through the "cracks" of our social infrastructure, a social infrastructure that was infinitely too thin to support his humanity.

Of course, there were some who wondered why he had ventured out into such uncertain circumstances. Some, for instance, wondered why he'd left his home, Honduras, for Brooklyn. Some wondered why he hadn't contacted members of his family, who were living in North Carolina at the time. Others, more pointedly, wondered why he hadn't heeded the signs that were put up around Prospect Lake, warning people to stay off the lake, to stay off the ice.

No one knows all the "whys" that led to his death. A few things we do know: before he died, he was without family; living in a shelter; no money; a foreigner in a foreign land.[2]

He was the wrong kind of person, in the wrong place, at the wrong time.

Whatever else you might say, he was walking on thin ice—and if you make that journey you take that chance.

I think the lawyer in Luke's Gospel knew a thing or two about reading signs, especially reading the danger signs around thin ice, about paying attention to the signs, or in this case, to the boundaries between safe and dangerous, wise and unwise.

And indeed, he should know the difference—knowing the difference was serious business, not to be taken lightly. Luke tells us that he was an expert in the law, an expert in how to keep covenant with the God of Israel, who the prophets tell us is a God of holy, consuming fire and a God of perfect, uncompromising justice. Even a passing knowledge of the judgment oracles of the prophets, and their "Thus saith the Lord," would be sufficient warning. If there ever was a patch of ice one needed to learn, it was this one: keeping the law of God in this world was no easy task, no mere curiosity; it could be and often was a question of life and death.

And so, the stakes are high when the expert in the law asks, "What must I do to inherit eternal life?"

Of course, the lawyer *knows* the law and when Jesus calls him on it he answers without missing a beat, almost like he was in a spelling bee and he was spelling the competition's winning word: "You shall love the Lord your God with all your heart, and with all your soul, and with all your strength, and with all your mind; and your neighbor as yourself."

"Good," says Jesus, "You have given the right answer; do this and you will live."

And the text tells us that the expert "wanted to justify himself." It may be that the questioner who had suddenly become the questioned

---

2. Kleinfield, "Through the Cracks, Then Through the Ice," *The New York Times*, February 1, 2004, sec. 1, 29.

sensed that he was being nudged in ways he did not have the courage to go, and he "wanted to justify himself"—which is to say, he sensed Jesus' original question, "How do you read it?," was asking not just for information but some indication of vocation.

There's a big difference between the two, vocation and information. To begin with, information is not, by itself, morally binding. Give me a little information, and I'm the better for it, maybe even dangerous, but that's it. I do with information what I please: I keep it, hide it, share it, use it, ignore it, file it, blog it, post it, delete it, suppress it, or shred it. I'm free to choose, according to my personal rule, which is more often than not the rule of my personal advantage. It's the idea that you get an education so you can get ahead, make a lot of money, but not much more.

Vocation, by contrast, involves something yet again. It involves living one's daily life not as one might necessarily choose, but as one ought, and this "ought" in Christian language is the rule of love. Paraphrasing Martin Luther, real freedom is nothing less than bondage to that which is greater than my personal advantage, even bondage to God's own self-giving love.

So, when the lawyer asks, "Who then is my neighbor? To whom am I obliged to show mercy?," he is moving, albeit reluctantly, from information to vocation, beyond what I know, what I choose, what I prefer, to the kind of person that I ought to be, the kind of person that God would make of me.

I say the expert makes that move from information to vocation reluctantly because he knows there are risks in vocation and he appears to be reading ice, in particular feeling for the thin places in Jesus' teaching, testing Jesus' knowledge to see if there were not some intrinsic weakness, some basic flaw that would fail disastrously for anyone who would follow him. It was a matter of survival, a matter of life and death. It's a serious dilemma.

You may recall, back in May of this year, the story of David Sharp, a man who had summited Mt. Everest, only to succumb to the elements on his descent. The debate, however, wasn't about his death, which wasn't at all unusual. The bodies of those who have died climbing Mt. Everest are clearly visible from the main trail: if you take that journey, you take that chance. What troubled the world's conscience, however, was that it was later learned that forty climbers passed Sharp while he was still alive.

Forty climbers decided he was a burden they could not afford to take on. Forty climbers chose to pass on the other side.

When people tried to explain his death they pointed to the obvious: he was ill prepared, lacking the proper gloves, and effectively dead. One might say he hadn't read the ice so well that day; he hadn't paid attention to the signage.

And for the forty climbers who passed him? Well, that was obvious: he was the wrong kind of person—*he was a liability*—in the wrong place—*in the death zone*, at the wrong time—*effectively dead, as they said, and, well, we're just about to summit . . . we were almost to our Jerusalem*.

And so in Jesus' parable, the Levite and the priest, two people who we would have expected to know the right thing to do, people who presumably knew the law, nevertheless pass on the other side, of this one who was effectively dead . . . and well, Jerusalem is just over the horizon.

Of course, we might excuse the Mt. Everest climbers more easily than we would the Levite and the priest . . . that is, part of the debate around David Sharp's death centered on the situation they were in, the death zone of Mt. Everest, the place where human life as we know it cannot be sustained for very long, even with the help of oxygen masks and the like. Their situation was extreme to say the least.

That may be, but the road between Jericho and Jerusalem was notoriously difficult, running for about seventeen miles, dropping thirty-four hundred feet. But it was not only the landscape that could be treacherous: in the fourth century, Jerome would describe the Jericho-Jerusalem road as one that was overrun with the criminal element. One who walked that road was walking in a veritable death zone.

One gets the sense that it wasn't the first time someone was left to die on that particular road, written off as effectively dead, just another victim, another bit of collateral damage.

Coincidently, as the world was debating the ethical character of the climbers who passed Sharp on their way to the summit, another climber, Lincoln Hall, was pronounced effectively dead. The news went out with little or no fanfare. People die on Mt. Everest: you make that journey, you take that risk. But then, just twelve hours after he was pronounced dead in the media, four other climbers who were themselves about to summit saw Hall—and he wasn't dead, but still alive. One of climbers described the surreal scene:

> Sitting to our left, about two feet from a 10,000 foot drop, was a man. Not dead, not sleeping, but sitting cross legged, in the process of changing his shirt. He had his down suit unzipped to the waist, his arms out of the sleeves, was wearing no hat, no gloves, no sunglasses, had no oxygen mask, regulator, ice axe, oxygen, no sleeping bag, no mattress, no food nor water bottle.

The four climbers abandoned their summit attempt and returned with Hall back down the mountain. Today, Lincoln Hall is fully recovered.[3]

Hall was liability in every possible way . . . but for the mercy he was shown, a mercy that was as risky as it was costly.

I don't know precisely what those climbers offered to Hall, but I wonder if they wouldn't recognize the Samaritan's actions as their own: the Samaritan made a detour from his intended journey, he bandaged and cleansed the man's wounds, gave up his own horse, cared for him, gave money to provide for his needs, and promised that he would not forget this man—in other words, he gave him a future when, at one time, his future was all but lost—this man who had been the wrong kind of person, in the wrong place, at the wrong time but for an improbable act of mercy.

So here we are, the United States of America, somewhere between the promised land of national security and the smoking wreckage of 9/11. It's a perilous road we are on, and there's plenty of collateral damage. Their hooded faces, their pleas for justice unheeded, mangled, tortured cries rising up out of secret prisons—we've seen them and heard them before, so many times that we might just be tempted to pass on the other side, where the ice is thicker, where the traveling is safer. And the burden of mercy . . . well, a little less costly, a lot less risky.

So we, at this university, are on our way, as students, faculty, administrators, trustees, somewhere on that sometimes treacherous road between Jericho and Jerusalem, somewhere between what we have been and what we aspire to be. It's a perilous road and there might even be a little collateral damage along the way.

It's not an easy place to be, there on that road, between Jericho and Jerusalem, no easy answers, just tough, sometimes costly, often risky decisions in the name of one's vocation, in the name of what one ought to be. Even so, while there might not be a lot of easy answers, the text today does suggest something of what those ethical decisions look like, maybe even

---

3. http://en.wikipedia.org/wiki/Lincoln_Hall_(climber), accessed on March 1, 2010.

something like loving kindness, seeking justice, and walking humbly—even into risky places, even into the death zone—with your God.

 . . . And besides, God is going there anyway, whether we, or our lawyers, advise it or not. That's where God has gone in Jesus Christ, out onto the thin ice, against all expert advice, yours and mine.

God is a bit wayward that way, heading off to the distant land, trotting off across the thin ice of the human condition. And whether we like it or not, God has shown, is showing, and will show mercy to a lot of people in the death zones of this world, people who have made bad decisions, people who haven't read the signs, people who are probably even the so-called wrong kind of people, maybe even our enemies, people who are liabilities to our purpose-driven world.

Maybe one or two of those wrong people are here today. Maybe you know something about living on thin ice, falling through the cracks. And more importantly, maybe you know something about the One who shows mercy . . . the One who binds up the brokenhearted and dwells with the contrite in spirit, the One who lifts up the downcast and downtrodden . . . maybe one or two of you were the wrong kind of people, in the wrong place, at the wrong time . . . wrong in every way but for the mercy of God. Amen.

October 26, 2006

4

The Day after Christmas

As a seminary professor, I am often sitting in the pew during the "high days" of the Christian year. Usually, in our line of work, we get the call from the local pastor who needs someone to fill the pulpit so that he or she can enjoy a well-deserved rest from preaching after the crush of Christmas or Easter. This sermon fits into that category, coming on the second Sunday of Christmas. The title of the sermon plays on the notion that there is a day and a day only for the celebration of Christ's birth and what he inaugurates. It also plays on the fairly common sentiment among some (and not necessarily just the Scrooges of Christmas) that Christmas comes to a timely end as we "return to normal." In a sense, I was attempting to employ the liturgical calendar as an indirect means of extending and deepening the church's embodiment of the Christmas message even as we "returned" to the normal rituals of daily living.

Of course, the nativity scene of Luke is hardly announcing the coming of either the normal or even "the new normal," whatever that means. Luke announces a new creation, a creation accompanied by a blast of trumpet and shout of song. But, having served as a Lamaze partner to my wife, Rebecca, I couldn't help but notice the absence of any account of Mary's suffering with child. This struck me as a startling omission until I began to sense that the songs of Elizabeth and Mary were somehow the way Luke recast the labor pains of birth that were part of the package for women after the fall. Isaiah's language that God pants and groans as a woman in labor also came to mind, layering my hearing of Luke's witness to the nativity with another tantalizing image of God's incarnation. Among the insights of exegetical work, I count this among one of my most cherished discoveries, that in Christ the labor of creation has become the song of the new thing of God.

Of course, it may be a wonderful image but sermons also have to do with the work of making people not merely poets—though making poets might well lead us to become better people. In any event, the reading from the epistle (Col. 3:12–17) seemed to introduce the more modest response of our daily life, making a decision to be a people of transformation, albeit in the lowercase decisions of an uppercase calling. Perhaps one could call this a kind of labor, the difficult decision to push against the grain of culture. With that in mind, I tried to bring back to mind the role of song amid the labors of life so that we might be emboldened to sing an unexpected song of promise.

THE DAY AFTER CHRISTMAS

Now every year [Jesus'] parents went to Jerusalem for the festival of the Passover. And when he was twelve years old, they went up as usual for the festival. When the festival was ended and they started to return, the boy Jesus stayed behind in Jerusalem, but his parents did not know it. Assuming that he was in the group of travelers, they went a day's journey. Then they started to look for him among their relatives and friends. When they did not find him, they returned to Jerusalem to search for him. After three days they found him in the temple, sitting among the teachers, listening to them and asking them questions. And all who heard him were amazed at his understanding and his answers. When his parents saw him they were astonished; and his mother said to him, "Child, why have you treated us like this? Look, your father and I have been searching for you in great anxiety." He said to them, "Why were you searching for me? Did you not know that I must be in my Father's house?" But they did not understand what he said to them. Then he went down with them and came to Nazareth, and was obedient to them. His mother treasured all these things in her heart. And Jesus increased in wisdom and in years, and in divine and human favor. (Luke 2:41–52)

. . . And Mary and Joseph both went to the Passover, and Jesus went, and Luke tells us that they went every year, for twelve years. And they weren't alone. According to Luke, they were with a "group of travelers"—it consisted of family and friends but it included others, too. All together making their way to one of the major celebrations of the Jewish calendar.

I imagine the road between Nazareth and Jerusalem was a little like an airport terminal during the holidays. A major airport like O'Hare, London Heathrow, or LAX. Everyone is traveling: cousins, uncles and aunts, grandparents, maybe even a few great grandparents, babies are crying, teenagers are necking, mommas nursing, toddlers toddling—people of every kind and nation, on the move, squeezed into a major artery of an annual pilgrimage—a group of travelers on their way to Jerusalem.

These journeys, we know they're exciting, but they can also be exhausting. Gwendoline, our two-year-old, when she's had enough of being out and about, will hold out her arms, meaning, "Pick me up," and repeat the words, "Home, now, home, now."

Maybe there were a few folks, Mary and Joseph among them, who, while they went to the Passover with enthusiasm, were now saying something like Gwendoline's "Home, now." Let's get back to normal, back to our lives—after all, the celebration was ended.

On Tuesday night, the day after Christmas, I stopped by my office at the University—*I was getting back to normal*—and on my way back to the car, I saw Dale, one of the security guards, the only other person there besides myself. As we passed, we said hello to one another, and then, as I was about to get into my car, I asked, "So did you have a Merry Christmas?"

"Yes," he said, and then with a growl added, "but I'm glad it's over with."

He's not the only one: a good friend of ours, without fail, takes down the Christmas tree straight away, not the day after Christmas, but on Christmas Day! He's glad it's over with and maybe even happier to get his living room back to normal.

We might not be that extreme, but most of us, sooner or later, will welcome the opportunity to get back to normal—after all, it's the day after Christmas, and the celebration is ended.

And that, in fact, is where we enter Luke's Gospel today—the day after the Passover celebration. People may not say it too loudly, but they're looking forward to getting back to normal.

This is not to say that they did not look forward to the Passover—to the contrary, they did. Like our Christmas, the Passover was a celebration that had deep roots in Jewish history. The word *Passover*, which is taken from the Hebrew *pesach*, means "to have compassion," "to protect," or "to deliver"—all referring to things that God did on behalf of their people when they were slaves in Egypt: God had *compassion* on them, hearing their cries against their oppressors. God *protected* them against Pharaoh's attempts to hurt and harm them. And God ultimately *delivered* them, making the Hebrews, who were once slaves, into a free people, no longer beholden to any but their God, who himself acted in freedom.

God's protection, compassion, and deliverance, each freely given—these acts, these verbs were the roots of not only their history as a people but their hope, their prayer as a nation.

So, we understand, there is a great love in and around the Passover celebration. And maybe we also understand that there is a feeling of exhaustion, emotional and otherwise, around that same celebration.

Like Dale, perhaps like you and me, it's Tuesday for them, the day after Passover, and they're glad to be getting back to normal.

***

Or they would have got back to normal if Jesus hadn't decided to remain in the temple. This surprises his parents, probably his extended family too, but in some ways, reading Luke's story of Jesus' infancy, the longest of any of the Gospels, it would be surprising if he did anything normal at all. One does not exactly walk away from Luke's story saying, "normal."

Exactly the opposite, actually. Consider Zechariah, who was the first to hear from Gabriel that something was up: he didn't quite appreciate that fact, and was stunned speechless for the duration of Elizabeth's pregnancy, and that was just the birth of John. When it came to Jesus' birth, words like "perplexed," "terrified," "amazed," pop up like pimples for a teenager—they're everywhere.

Even more, upon hearing of Jesus' birth, people start bursting out in song, even old man Zechariah learns to sing, and Mary and Elizabeth too.

And this is curious to me, maybe it is to you too, something that is not in any of the Gospel stories about Jesus' birth:

We never hear about the labor pains that Mary went through,

Only her songs.

Having been present for the birth of our two daughters, having heard other moms giving birth down the hall from us, crying out with everything they've got, every muscle and hair follicle joining the cause, every ounce of will, every tear of resistance, everything and more than that, summoned to join the cause of childbirth—one thinks that at least one of the Gospels, even if they were written by thick-headed men, would at least make a note, even a footnote, on the nature of this birth, in particular how the mother labored with this child.

But we don't get that—what we do get are songs: impulsive, spontaneous, audacious songs that burst off the page into "Glorias" and "hallelujahs" and praise—almost as though the songs that they sing are the songs of the Lord, who in Isaiah, "pants and gasps" like a woman in labor, in labor with the New Thing of God.

Could it be that even the labor pains of Mary have been written over, transformed by the holy gasping and panting of God's coming into the world, summoning to himself a stunning chorus of praise, a chorus of irrepressible, unashamed, audacious, irresistible praise, singing God's New Creation into the world?

Singing praise where only pain had been known before . . .

***

Praise, the unusual word—unusual in this world, where the cries of humanity are more often strangled by pain than liberated by praise—

Unusual in a world more accustomed to hunger than happiness,

More acquainted with war than peace,

More familiar with songs of sadness than with shouts of joy.

But Jesus, the unusual child . . . the unusual son of Mary.

He stayed in the temple. Never told his parents where he was. Probably didn't think twice about it. And I don't think it was a case of adolescent rebellion, as some might interpret it, but it was simply Jesus being Jesus. He stayed in the temple, even after the crowds, including his family, friends, and relatives, had finished with the celebration and were busy getting home, getting back to life as usual.

But for Jesus, the unusual child, the unusual son of Mary, there was no such thing as the day after Christmas . . . or at least there was nothing like "getting back to normal."

And it's possible that even though Luke tells us that Jesus was "obedient" to Mary and Joseph, they knew it too: everything had changed, and nothing would or could ever be the same.

But still, Jesus went with them back to Nazareth. And so also Jesus goes with us, to our Nazareth of the Normal, whatever and wherever that may be. Even the day after Christmas, the unusual child, the unusual Word in the world, he joins us.

And it is also possible that the little child who joins us is also the little child who leads us on this familiar road, teaching us on the way about what it means to be his people, an unusual people in a world where pain seems more common than praise.

✻✻✻

Colossians 3, part of today's lectionary readings, offers some unusual words for us to live by:

In a world where it is normal for people to be naked in their anger and hostility toward each other, clothe yourselves with compassion.

In a world where it is normal and even applauded if you hold grudges, and never forgive, instead you should bear with one another and, if you have a complaint against another, forgive each other, just as the Lord has forgiven you.

In a world where it is normal to shiver in the loneliness of our inhumanity, clothe yourselves with love, for love binds everything together in perfect harmony.

Unusual words inspired by an unusual child, the unusual son of Mary.

Sooner or later, if we haven't already, we'll join Mary and the other travelers on the way back to Nazareth: the Christmas decorations will be boxed up, the tree put out on the curb, the recycling bins filled with boxes and wrapping paper, the nativity scene and the inflatable snowman will be collected off the front lawn and stowed away in the attic—the silly and the sacred together, surrendered to the call to get back to normal.

So it is with us, and so it was with Mary. But I wonder whether Mary, on that familiar road back to Nazareth, whether she did not feel the ache of a still-distant sadness growing near—and maybe she sang a little bit, where sadness might have been, sang in a quiet sort of way, singing with words too deep for words, something like the way we might sing: Joy to the world, the Lord is come, let earth receive her king . . .

Amen.

Westminster Presbyterian Church
Galena, Illinois
December 31, 2006

5

Our Greatest Possession

JUST BEFORE PROCESSING INTO chapel for the 2006 baccalaureate service where I was to preach, I tried to explain to a colleague my hopes for this sermon. I said the sermon was meant as a "benediction for the graduating class." As a baccalaureate sermon, I wanted to express God's promise and presence as our students began the long journey of congregational service. On a less pious note, this class was also the first I had watched grow from orientation week to graduation day. After all my demands upon them as a teacher, many of them unreasonable (especially in retrospect), I owed them an expression of gratitude, if not, in some instances, an apology. This was not the time to "exhort" but, rather, to announce God's promise to be with us.

But I soon found announcing benediction amid the troubles of the church seemed somehow disingenuous. The "church in crisis" is an almost constant companion to seminary life, where we regularly hear about membership decline, contemporary and social irrelevance, biblical and theological illiteracy, divisions, and bickering between factions. Pronouncing benediction over this often dismal scene seemed a bit much; pronouncing it on those about to enter into that mess seemed evasive if not dishonest. And yet, this is precisely what the church does on the Lord's Day, at the end of each service, raising benedictory hands over a community that has its fair share of bruises and setbacks.

At the level of theology, I was puzzled by the paradox, pronouncing benediction amid troubles—as puzzled as any pastor who hears benediction not only as a good word to part with but a promise to live by. As I was reflecting on this particular problem, an episode from John Steinbeck's

East of Eden came back to me, where Samuel explains why he named his moody, swaybacked horse, "Doxology," or "Dox" for short. Steinbeck's image of the horse and its name is profound and was more than enough to help me negotiate the tension between the church as it is and the church as God's elected (and benedicted) community.

Perhaps what I attempted to evoke in this sermon was a species of doxology, or praise of God, that we frequently overlook. Specifically, what I aimed for was an evocation of what Hughes Oliphant Old describes as an *epicletic doxology*: ". . . [T]he word *epiclesis* means to 'call upon, to make an appeal to someone or address oneself to someone.' When the faithful call upon God in time of need, God is glorified. The very act of calling upon God's name is itself worship."[1] Knowing that our students would pass through seasons of life and ministry when the song of praise seemed distant, I hoped to name the act of epiclesis, or calling on God, as a way they could glorify God when they felt most ill-equipped to offer such praise. More importantly, perhaps, I aimed to remind the church that its sole gift is to reflect God's glory, a living, active presence in a world all too acquainted with suffering.

OUR ONE GREAT POSSESSION

O sing to the LORD a new song, sing to the LORD all the earth. Sing to the LORD, bless his name; tell of his salvation from day to day. (Ps. 96:1-2)

In the beginning was the Word, and the Word was with God, and the Word was God. He was in the beginning with God. All things came into being through him, and without him not one thing came into being. What has come into being in him was life, and the life was the light of all people. The light shines in the darkness, and the darkness did not overcome it.

There was a man sent from God, whose name was John. He came as a witness to testify to the light, so that all might believe through him. He himself was not the light, but he came to testify to the light. The true light which enlightens everyone was coming into the world.

He was in the world, and the world came into being through him; yet the world did not know him. He came to what was his own, and his own people did not accept him. But to all who received him, who believed in his

---

1. Old, *Themes and Variations for a Christian Doxology*, 17.

name, he gave power to become children of God, who were born, not of blood or of the will of the flesh or of the will of man, but of God.

And the Word became flesh and lived among us, and we have seen his glory, the glory as of a father's only son, full of grace and truth.
(John 1:1–14)

Many of you are familiar with John Steinbeck's *East of Eden*, a book that even in its title suggests a rich exploration of theological and biblical themes. Especially memorable in this regard is a passage about an old cranky horse named Doxology, or simply "Dox" for short. Samuel, his owner, is questioned about the horse, and in particular his name, which makes no sense given the horse's just-this-side-of-dog-food condition. Surprisingly, instead of defending the horse, Samuel agrees that Dox is not what he used to be; indeed, he never was what he was supposed to be:

> "Everything was wrong with him . . . [then just as now]. He's hammerheaded and swaybacked. . . . I have never in thirty-three years found one good thing about him. . . . He is selfish and quarrelsome and mean and disobedient. . . . When I feed him . . . he tries to bite my hand. And I love him."
>
> . . . "And you named him Doxology?"
>
> "Surely," said Samuel, "so ill endowed a creature deserved, I thought, one grand possession."
>
> . . . "Maybe you should put him out of his misery."
>
> "What misery?" Samuel demanded. "He's one of the few happy and consistent beings I've ever met."
>
> "He must have aches and pains."
>
> "Well, he doesn't think so. Doxology still thinks he's one hell of a horse."[2]

Doxology, our doxology, the church's doxology—so disguised by conceits and failures, aches and pains, that some struggle to see it, much less to hear it.

But you, the graduating class, are different. As seminarians, you have not only seen Doxology for what it is, you've gone even further and indicated you will be "married" to this strangely beloved, curmudgeonly old creature.

---

2. Adapted from Steinbeck's *East of Eden*, 303–04.

You may love the church, but hopefully yours is not a blind love. By this time, you know Doxology is not necessarily what it was cracked up to be. Fact is, you've heard a train of speakers and preachers, dignitaries and officials, professors and practitioners each tell you from pulpit and lectern that the church is in trouble. For three, maybe four years you've heard this message or something like it: the church is hemorrhaging, it's going to split, it is divided by sectarian jealousies and ugly controversies, it is unkind, even mean-spirited to its pastors. And not to put too fine a point on it, most pastors aren't all they were cracked up to be either: gossipers, adulterers, split by jealousies and driven by envies, and frankly not even that accomplished in their given craft. You know the litany of trouble, like you know your own hand.

Your friends, family, associates, they're all here today, and I'm sure they come with their support and prayers. But at one point or another, they're going to ask you, if they haven't already: Why bother? Life is short. Don't waste what is so precious on that which is so ugly. And it won't be the first time you've heard the question, because long before anyone else posed the question, you asked it of yourself: Why bother?

Maybe you don't know. Maybe you don't have the courage to leave. After all, you've invested time, resources, and energy into this thing. Or it could be that you're just stupid. Maybe you're just as stubborn and thick-headed as the church is . . . you were made for each other . . .

Maybe that's it. But I doubt it. I guess I don't think anyone was *made* for the church, stupid or not. *Called to* the church, yes; *made for*, no.

I think there's something more here, and it has something to do with the name that the church has been given and the One who has given it; it has to do with what the church has always been; and it has to do with what the church has already become by God's grace in Jesus Christ.

The name that the church has been given: *We've been given a name.* And with that name we have been called. The name *Doxology* belongs to the church only because the church belongs to God. When we sing the Doxology, we sing it in the knowledge of its *absolute givenness*. There's no other way to sing it. If you sing it as though you own it, like it was part of your religious portfolio, even if you hit every note just right, you have not sung Doxology. Truth be known, the only thing right about us, the only thing redemptive in us, the single solitary redemptive good thing in us is, ironically, not us but Christ who gives himself, his own presence to be beneath us, above us, before us, behind us, beside us, and, almost beyond belief, Christ himself is given to be within us. We have been called to be the body of Christ, and out of that vocational identity, an identity that is given, we sing the church's Doxology.

What the church has always been . . . well that's painfully evident, isn't it? If the church is not being persecuted from the outside, it is doing a pretty good job of cannibalizing itself.

Sometimes I think our problem is the lighting. Maybe we ought to have the owner of *those* establishments in downtown East Dubuque come by, pay them as consultants, have them explain what to do with the light, or what *not* to do with it. Maybe they'd suggest keeping it off the customers, keep them in the shadows, preserve the safety of their anonymity, allow them to cluster into even darker corners with their friends, their hurts, their hungers. Only turn on the lights after hours.[3]

I imagine there are a few of us who'd like to keep the lights dimly lit, especially when the "customers" are around. Problem with this is that I don't think God gives us that option. John, for his part, is pretty convinced that God's light has come into the world in Jesus Christ.

It's even possible that the light of Jesus Christ even leaks into the church every once in a while . . . and even if it is just a trickle of that light, that light which is the true light, that lights up everything that comes into the world—in that light even the darkest church gives up its shadows, yours and mine.

When light leaks into the church like that, you might think we were just exposed, naked to judgment, to ridicule, and shame. That's the way light works most of the time. It works either to make you into a spectacle of praise or a spectacle for someone else's abuse. But that's a different kind of light.

The light we're talking about is the light that has come into the world, God's glory dwelling among us full of grace and truth. It's the kind of light that wraps its warmth around you, like a garment so rich and pure and compassionate and holy and beautiful that there is no shadow of turning, no shadow of shame, no impurity that is not cleansed, no wound that is not healed, and no tomb that is not opened into the abundance of resurrection life. I think that's why Paul Tillich said that the church waits for what it already has: light has come into the world, and we have *beheld* the glory of the only begotten of the Father, the one who so loved the world. . .

---

3. The reference to "*those* establishments in . . . East Dubuque" is a reference to Dubuque's sex industry.

. In other words, today we know that the downcast and the brokenhearted have already become, by God's grace in Jesus Christ, a living witness to God's reign on earth.

I guess as far as I'm concerned, that's permission enough to sing, to sing without apology or embarrassment, to exult in the name that we have been given.

So go ahead, church, keep singing the song that you have been given. Sing it out loud, roll your shoulders to its rhythm, sing it in the quiet of your heart, and early in the morning, and again at the setting of the sun, sing it once more in that helpless, sleepless, hapless hour, and sing it again, and again, and again—your one grand possession . . . buried in the hearts of the least, the last, and the lost.

Sing your song . . . and keep singing it, for as long as you can. The world needs to hear it. *We need to hear it.*

But listen:

If there ever comes a day when you know your troubles by heart—

> the jealousies, the betrayals, the disappointments, the conceits, the lies, some your own,
>
> some belonging to others—

If there ever comes a day when you know your troubles by heart,

> but for your life, you can't remember your name,
>
> > can't remember your song . . .

Would you do something, if that day ever comes?

Would you be still for a moment?

> Be still with trouble,
>
> Be still with the aches and the betrayals,
>
> Be still in the futility of trying . . .

Be still even as Doxology is still. What else can you do, what else can we do? But be still . . . and wait . . . for the one who called you, for the one who named you, for the Lord who loves you with an everlasting love . . . the Lord will send another to sing for you, the Spirit to sing within you, God will send the earth and the stars, and all the oceans of the sea, and every mountain, and you will remember, by God's grace, *we* will remember our name that was buried, but is now risen, our life that was lost, but now is found. And we will know together, just as the waters cover the sea, that the Lord is near . . . upon our lips and within our hearts, even deep, almost irretrievably deep in the hearts of the least, the last, and the lost.

Doxology . . . our one great possession, the one thing that we have to give, perhaps the only thing we have to give. So let us give it as it was given to us: with love, with abandon, with compassion, with peace, with mercy, with hope . . . everlasting. Amen.

May 12, 2006

PART TWO

EQUIPPING

I

WE SEE TEACHERS WALKING briskly to their classes, a few minutes late, a clutch of photocopied articles in one hand, textbooks in another, and, perhaps, a grade book. Unlike "movers and shakers," their shoes do not often bear the high-gloss shine of success but, rather, the dull, mud-like glow of anxious neglect. Between their lateness and their handouts, they have a lecture, one that seems, at least in their own estimation, woefully inadequate for the coming hour. And yet, inadequate or not, students are ready, they are waiting, some with anticipation, others grudgingly or maybe distracted by other matters. Perhaps they pass the time chatting with one another, until the professor steps behind the lectern, arranges his or her notes, and, in one way or another, calls the assembly to order. Behind that hurried pace to class, there were staff and committee meetings, frustrations with a lack of funding as well as with a larger culture, both in the church and Western society, that views education and educators in a less than flattering light.

A teacher, it seems to me, walks a lonely path, especially as he or she is stereotyped by generalized views of incompetence, being seen as fumbling, careless in dress, eccentric, and ineffective. The saying, "Those who can't do, teach," captures the skeptical view of educators that seems to prevail among some. From this perspective, teachers seem a bit like the "stinktree" described by Thomas Merton, a tree so twisted and full of knots as to be useless in a world more interested in product than process:

> No carpenter will even look at [the stinktree].
> Such is your teaching—
> Big and useless.[1]

Poets, too, seem useless to most "high-octane" performers as well, perhaps explaining in part why the words of poets are so often to be found in the workplaces of teachers. The poet evokes the soul of the teacher, according to Sam M. Intrator, their words often scattered, almost randomly, but never carelessly, throughout the teacher's world:

> The poems lie folded in the hidden corners of a teacher's wallet. They are taped to the computer or pinned on a corkboard next to the teacher's desk. Or clipped inside a grading book or written on the cover of a planning binder. Sometimes they are written out in flowing calligraphy and get central billing in the front of a classroom or on the door as a special sign of welcome.[2]

Tucked away, posted like mastheads of wisdom in a world of folly, taped to the wall as outposts of sanctuary, wherever these words appear one may well find the habitat of a teacher or, indeed, a pastor.

So far as I can tell, poetry and the people who write it have yet to find their niche in the global economy, and perhaps, by God's grace, they never will. They appear to be notoriously ill-equipped for a world preoccupied with developing revenue streams. Perhaps that is why poets still speak wisdom. In my life as a student, I savored these literary gems, as I wandered outside faculty offices, often passing my time by reading the poetry my professors had posted outside their offices, witty sayings and wise insights from John Donne or Emily Dickinson, a quip from a C. S. Lewis or a G. K. Chesterton. I loved those corkboard messages, sometimes scribbling an especially memorable insight onto a scrap of paper, one that I could not bear to leave unsavored, unremembered. Mostly, though, I did not write them down, but looked forward to seeing them again, like familiar friends. Many of these friends were old, paper yellow with years, seemingly forgotten, though still emblazoned there for all who cared to see, to hear, to remember. For me, their words blazed like oracular fire,

---

1. Merton, *The Way of Chuang Tzu*, 35.
2. Intrator, *Stories of the Courage to Teach*, xiii.

illuminating the drab space of a teacher, mostly forgotten by the institutional preoccupations of higher education.

Of course, while poetry may decorate the teacher's habitat, that does not always mean their lives abound with poetic expressions. Rather the opposite, as Intrator, a college professor, reminds us:

> If the poets' words were languorous, gentle, and contoured, ours were charged, careening, and jagged. The poet described her work as contemplative. We described our work as a crazy quilt of roles and tasks. If the poet strolls forth taking the world in, the teacher bustles about trying to create those high-octane connections between students, subject matter, and teacher.[3]

Pastors, too, might recognize this tension: the love of language and the "crazy quilt of roles and tasks" associated with doing ministry.

And yet, unlike many teachers who labor in the trenches of committee and classroom enduring years of famine, pastors as well as seminary professors regularly participate in the life of worship, where we, as a people, feast on the word proclaimed. Laboring over a text, being absorbed by it or inhabiting its life, we begin to digest the nutrient-dense word, its presence reaching into the marrow through proclamation. I like to think that chapel sermons could, in a similar way to the poetry we sometimes see tacked or taped to the teacher's door, become a familiar friend of the seminary community, refreshing students, faculty, and staff with a reminder as well as a remembrance, a moment when, during the time-driven day, the seminary community can leave the "charged, careening, and jagged" edge of the classroom and enter into the liturgically familiar, often poetic patterns of worship.

II

Sometimes a professor begins her or his class with a call and response more familiar to the life of worship than to the life of the classroom:

> The Lord be with you.
>
> *And also with you.*

Why? Why use language more characteristic of worship than academic inquiry? I suppose part of the reason appears as we reflect on the

---

3. Ibid., 2.

journey that brought us to the classroom in the first place. When we hear these words, or the words of prayer, the seminary classroom remembers the imprint of faith that it bears, acknowledging that its life of inquiry is not, as someone has written, understanding in a desperate search for faith but faith in search of deeper understanding. Words of liturgy and prayer, worn smooth by repetition, remind the classroom—student and teacher—of its life in communion.

Yet, if this is so, a curious irony begins to surface, namely around chapel attendance . . . or the lack thereof. True, most, if not all, seminary students thirst for the primary language of worship—their appetite or hunger for worship steels each student for the demands of theological education. And some would probably say that their thirst for theological education was itself traceable to an experience in worship. So, not surprisingly, like the sacrament of the Lord's Supper, most would agree that we need worship frequently, so often that we come to recognize it as an integral expression of theological education. And yet, that sentiment belies a common reality: some students, as well as faculty and staff, view what happens in chapel as less than integral to theological education, concluding that it is more elective than constitutive of the seminary experience.

To be fair, sometimes decisions to "drop" chapel reflect not so much a low view of worship as they do the high level of content, social and academic, that characterizes seminary life. Sometimes I think the social obligations (particularly in a small seminary) to be in fellowship together are at least as significant as the academic requirements. Among the many "good things" that characterize seminary life, a few will always reason that something has to go, and sometimes that means either reducing or eliminating chapel as a part of their seminary experience.

I know that temptation personally and have succumbed to it often enough. But why? Why do people who profess to believe that worship expresses the most important part of being human decide that chapel, of all things, can be viewed as more elective than constitutive? And particularly in seminary, where we equip people to serve as worship leaders, where we are constantly reminded in the classroom of the patterns of worship, how do we come to decide that chapel is not integral to the classroom? What takes place in the reasoning process that leads students to say, "Studying for my church history exam is more important than attending daily worship"? The same could be said of teachers, who, usually ordained, say something similar, differing only in perspective but not in substance.

Some might answer these questions by saying that the Lord's Day fulfills our obligations to gather for worship, thereby eliminating the need for weekday chapel. The Lord's Day, they might say, expresses the primary point of reference for our worshiping life and that chapel is, at best, an "extra" for those who want it or need it. Another criticism of chapel targets not so much chapel as it does seminary life itself: faculty, students, and staff feel as if there is more and more to do with fewer and fewer resources, human and institutional. But in some ways, the deeper question appears not in our relative workload, but in the tension between work and worship. For seminaries dedicated to the "good work" of theological education, the tension may even be more pronounced.

III

From my experience, seminaries seem almost bipolar regarding their identification with the church, some appearing to view it is an embarrassment, others electing to remain aloof from anything that smacks of congregational life, or, by contrast, overidentifying with the church, such that legitimate distinctions and appropriate functions between theological education and the local church seem to blur. But what, at heart, is the source of this tension? Where does it come from? And why is that tension so pronounced relative to chapel?

My own answer to this question goes to the way corporate worship, especially during the weekday, seems like an intrusion into an educational system that frequently, despite its best efforts, focuses more intently on product than process.

I liken the tension to something I experience when taking my daughters sledding in the winter: while my daughters seem thoroughly absorbed in the process, I am focused almost exclusively on the destination. From the point of getting the girls dressed and safely secured in their car seats, to arriving at the hill, I am worrying whether or how long we will stay on the hill: "Will it be worth all the effort of getting them in their snow outfits? Will they step out of the car, and in less than five minutes, whine that it is too cold, 'I want to go home!'?"—something they almost invariably do.

Even so, all the while as I am going through these scenarios more related to product and destination (what we actually accomplish), the girls act in ways symptomatic of their absorption by the process, occupied by countless, myriad "distractions" (as I see them) of dressing and relating ("I want these socks!" "Gwen's not being nice to me!"), to walking the short distance from the back door of our home to the car, kicking piles of snow, ambling off down the driveway, belaboring an otherwise short journey with countless detours and pit stops that, in my "production"-oriented mentality, could be happily eliminated.

Sometimes chapel looks like this: more process than product.

And arguing the point becomes strained. After all, the student who decides that chapel will probably not help him or her in the church history exam tells a truth with which we would be hard pressed to argue: twenty minutes in chapel does not usually produce the kind of knowledge required for an "A" in a church history exam. It seems a "waste" of time. However, beyond not contributing to the "bottom line" of our educational endeavors, the life of worship actually *delights* in what Marva Dawn calls a "royal waste of time." Chapel intrudes regularly and without apology. "Worship," she asserts, "ought not to be construed in a utilitarian way. Its purpose is not to gain numbers nor for our church to be seen as successful. Rather, the entire reason for our worship is that God deserves it."[4] Likewise, within the seminary chapel, the actions of gathering, proclaiming, responding, and sending around a biblical witness may be (and often will be) irrelevant to our immediate work. However, if it is "waste," it is paradoxical waste: those irrelevant patterns summon out of us unusual focus, leading people to dance down the aisles, to sing robustly the songs of faith, and sometimes moving people to laughter and tears in a work world otherwise unfamiliar and even uncomfortable with such all-too-human expressions.

We might designate this phenomenon as the sanctification of time, turning what otherwise might be a mean-spirited preoccupation with product into the generosity evident in a community born of worship.

We can probably do no better than recall John's account of Mary anointing Jesus: "Mary took a pound of costly perfume made of pure nard, anointed Jesus' feet, and wiped them with her hair. The house was filled with the fragrance of the perfume" (John 12:3–4). Another text, this one from the Old Testament, evokes a similar image of an abundance that overwhelms the merely good with the holy: "The house, the house of the Lord, was filled with a cloud so that the priests could not stand to minister

---

4. Dawn, *A Royal Waste of Time*, 1.

because of the cloud; for the glory of the Lord filled the house of God" (2 Chron. 5:13b–14).

Both texts provide fascinating perspectives for thinking about the relationship between worship and work. Although we habitually take a dim view of Judas Iscariot, he tells an indisputable truth even if, according to John, he was double minded: Mary's act of worship was irrelevant to the crying needs of the poor. Mary embodied an inexplicable departure from the "product"-oriented mentality of the church—she became absorbed in the process. But interestingly enough, her absorption in that act of worship "filled the house" with its fragrance; her act, then, was not narcissistic but, rather, sublimely communal, so that no one, not even the product-oriented Judas Iscariot, could escape from the strange presence of that seemingly frivolous waste.

The theophany of 2 Chronicles 5:11–14 reveals something similar, though this time without the "double-mindedness" of Judas Iscariot to obscure our view. Without any ambiguity whatsoever, the chronicler reminds us that the priests were doing a good work, the work of worship. Yet, God disrupts their good work. A fair question for the church and its institutions of theological education to ask might be this: How often do we prop up our "good work" as sufficient and therefore all-encompassing? God's disruption, filling the house of the Lord with the darkness of divine light, brings us back not to our senses, even our best sense, but, rather to our faith. Indeed, the rite and liturgy of worship, the instruments and songs of praise first stammer and then falter altogether as the community finds itself surrounded by God's glory.

Perhaps one of the more important lessons of chapel is not how well it serves our good work or our needs but, rather, the way sometimes the Spirit uses chapel to sanctify our work, interrupting it with something like useless and indulgent play, profoundly irrelevant and for that reason, all the more transformative. It is a lesson we do not master in a semester or in a year, or in many years, or even in a lifetime. Perhaps the seminary chapel plays a part in accentuating that ongoing lesson in human development, insinuating useless worship into the meritocracy of education, gently subverting its preoccupation with scarcity with the rich, even ludicrous abundance of sacrament.

IV

The word *companion* comes to mind as I think about the relationship between chapel and classroom, having within it the etymological roots of "com" (community) and "pan" (bread). We recently purchased a hand-operated wheat mill and I am coming to appreciate with great depth the actual labor of making bread. Among other things, it is time consuming as well as labor intensive. Grinding wheat berries reminds me that the final product, bread, was born, at least in part, from the application of muscle and sweat, something in the era of "wonder" bread we can easily forget. Using the wheat mill, by contrast, reminds me of the hard work of bread making, which has obvious analogies with the work of theological education: writing papers, reading books, lectures, and more forms of assessment and accountability than anyone would actually want—these can seem like a sojourn in the desert.

And yet, despite all this work, whenever a loaf comes out of the oven, the yeast doing its invisible but sacred work, something almost magical occurs when we finally witness the hard, indigestible wheat berries we once sweated over transformed into rich, airy, aromatic bread. When it comes out of the oven, everyone wants a slice, lathered with butter and jam, fat and sweetness melting together—and the spirit of that house becomes one not of work but of celebration. This certainly suggests the feeling on graduation day, as the community witnesses students receiving affirmation for their hard work. One senses a great abundance in that moment, a surplus of joy, not measurable by work alone.

It would, however, be too long to wait until graduation for this feast: chapel worship can be something like the warm invasion of the Spirit, as the preacher of the day breaks open the word, steaming hot, fresh out of the oven of the pastoral imagination, evoking something rich and inexplicable in the community of scholars. The whole community alike could be said to be in the business of grinding wheat and kneading dough, tending to the laborious work of theological study—but there is always something more than our labors, infinitely more, and chapel, the richness of liturgy and shared worship, brings us into the abundant joy of the Spirit at play.

6

The Most True Thing

THE WORK OF ASSESSMENT generates an almost constant hum in higher education and, in some instances, can become one of its most tragic characteristics. My own bias developed early, when, as a rising fifth grader, I saw my younger brother, in tears, on the last day of school. He held his report card in hand, a card that said he was being held back, kept in the third grade. I suppose what the card said was that my brother needed remedial work. At the time, we did not know what dyslexia meant and I am not sure our teachers did either. None of it mattered, anyway: what my brother heard was that he was a failure. I doubt he ever overcame that blow entirely and it saddens me even now, remembering his soul crushed so needlessly and senselessly, cutting him from a community that he counted as friends, cutting out a part of his identity in the name of assessment.

One might guess, and correctly, that I come to my present vocation with ambivalence toward assessment-oriented work. Obviously, one expects the assessment of student work. Assessment forms an undeniably significant, and important, part of seminary education. However, the growth of an "assessment culture" threatens to become almost perverse. Sometimes theological education seems to exist at the center of a veritable storm of assessment-oriented criteria: some of those criteria are developed by the Association of Theological Schools (ATS); others are developed by faculty for promotion and tenure; and still others are developed within academic divisions. And, of course, the syllabi name criteria for assessment: papers, sermons, group projects, written exams, and so on. Even coming to seminary is a process of achieving minimum standards for admission beyond mere academic readiness: maturity of one's sense of call; theological articulateness; affirmation of call by members of the faith community as well as those outside that immediate community.

Assessment is not all bad, of course. Some of my greatest strides as a teacher happened as a result of thoughtful feedback from students, peers, and supervisors. Without candid and constructive critique from the community we are not likely to grow either in our personhood or as God's beloved community. Students, too, grow through feedback that contributes to a learning environment. Without assessment the church itself suffers: ministers benefit from regular reviews of their work. But why so much assessment? Part of the answer resides in the challenges of ministry: ministry isn't easy work. Pastoring and preaching requires from us the sensitivity of the counselor, the savvy of an administrator, the gifts of the poet, and the vision of a leader. Who possesses all these gifts? Sometimes we take comfort in the notion that we may enjoy one spiritual gift, but even that one suffers if the others are either inadequate or neglected. Serving the church requires not only good intentions but real results. We also see the growing challenges of serving in a changing world. Somehow or other, we need to review our efforts, recalibrate, and commit to growth, personal and vocational.

Even so, the constant "hum" of assessment is everywhere and I worry that the good it intends sometimes diminishes the work of theological education as a whole. What distinguishes mere hazing from constructive criticism? The short answer is love, God's love. The active presence of love, a love that leavens the critical work of assessment with formative nurture, changes not only how we "do" assessment but the spirit with which we receive it and pursue change. Of course, when we come to the biblical text itself, we find no shortage of assessment, only this time it comes in the biblical lexicon of judgment.

I puzzled over this question of assessment in the following sermon, delivered at a chapel service at the beginning of a summer intensive course. The text assigned for that day was Mark's account of the rich man who comes to Jesus asking what more he may need to do to be acceptable for the kingdom. The text triggered in me an imaginative response to a problem that seemed relevant to people who sometimes struggle with the nature of their calling: What happened to the rich man in the Gospel after he walked away from Jesus, his report card in his hand? To answer that question, I chose to play with our preoccupation with assessment in academic culture, tweaking it a bit with what I see as the overriding preoccupation of God in Jesus Christ: steadfast, unequivocal, determined, never-to-be-swayed, unapologetic love. This sermon represents my attempt to put the culture of assessment in an appropriately theological frame of reference. Despite our best intentions, constant assessment without loving affirmation can turn into little more than getting our "pound of flesh" as we eat each other alive; chapel preaching can offer a countervailing witness to our tendency toward cannibalism.

Pastorally, I wanted to try to defuse some of the gnawing doubts that eat away at students, particularly in their first year of seminary. As they confront the first tidal wave of papers and assignments, as they are bowled over by the sheer mass of readings, and then as they are either humbled or exalted by grades and evaluations, students, like any of us, can struggle to hold on to why they came to seminary in the first place, why they responded to God's call in their life. My hope for those who heard this sermon was that they would frame the culture of assessment with the assessment that makes everything worthwhile: God's turning the culture of assessment upside down with grace, love, and mercy, "the most true thing" we should ever know about ourselves or the world in which we live.

THE MOST TRUE THING

As [Jesus] was setting out on a journey, a man ran up and knelt before him, and asked him, "Good teacher, what must I do to inherit eternal life?" Jesus said to him, "Why do you call me good? No one is good but God alone. You know the commandments: 'You shall not murder; You shall not commit adultery; You shall not steal; You shall not bear false witness; You shall not defraud; Honor your father and mother.'" He said to him, "Teacher, I have kept all these since my youth." Jesus, looking at him, loved him and said, "You lack one thing; go, sell what you own, and give the money to the poor, and you will have treasure in heaven; then come, follow me." When he heard this, he was shocked and went away grieving, for he had many possessions.

Then Jesus looked around and said to his disciples, "How hard it will be for those who have wealth to enter the kingdom of God!" And the disciples were perplexed at these words. But Jesus said to them again, "Children, how hard it is to enter the kingdom of God! It is easier for a camel to go through the eye of a needle than for someone who is rich to enter the kingdom of

God." They were greatly astounded and said to one another, "Then who can be saved?" Jesus looked at them and said, "For mortals it is impossible, but not for God; for God all things are possible."

Peter began to say to him, "Look, we have left everything and followed you." Jesus said, "Truly I tell you, there is no one who has left house or brothers or sisters or mother or father or children or fields, for my sake and for the sake of the good news, who will not receive a hundredfold now in this age—houses, brothers and sisters, mothers and children, and fields with persecutions—and in the age to come eternal life. But many who are first will be last, and the last will be first." (Mark 10:17–31)

A lot of ink has spilled on the question of this rich man's reaction to Jesus, especially regarding what he eventually did with his grief and shock: Did he ultimately give away his wealth? Or did he choose to keep his wealth and his misery with it? Did he live the rest of his life in the comfort of his Cadillac or did he wander off to some biblical version of Calcutta to serve the poor?

Whatever we imagine the outcome of his part in the story of Jesus, it is fair to say that we don't often think of him as an especially promising candidate for the kingdom of God. After all, the last time we saw him, he left Jesus and the company of disciples in a state of "shock and grief." That was his exit interview with the Lord Jesus. And that was the last of him. We never hear of him again in the Gospel of Mark.

But what if, just for the sake of conversation, he came back, wanting a second interview with Jesus, and he came to you, to ask you for a letter of reference, a recommendation?

Maybe he heard you had enrolled in seminary. And now people are saying you know a few things. And maybe it's true. You do know a few things. You're fatigued but flush with the wisdom of the divines. And it's not just you. It's us too. Faculty, staff, and administrators. Especially at the beginning of the semester. We're shiny people. Glowing people. Loving people. Praying people. Preaching people. Maybe by December it'll be different, but now things smell rosy. And what's more, for all of our loving and preaching and praying, we also like appreciation now and again . . . and this young man, he seems to have some sense. Maybe he got whiff of us as we were on our way to Greek this morning, and his depravity was awakened by the scent of our divinity.

And so he comes to us, sniffing us out, seeking our unction for a holy function. Maybe you're flattered by this attention. I know I would be. I'm grateful when people acknowledge my many talents and gifts. It compliments my humility nicely. So you're glad, but before you become too intoxicated by this welcome recognition, you remember how this privileged person, this silver-spoon-still-stuck-in-his-mouth person, you remember how he left Jesus in the Gospel of Mark—and with that sobering image in your mind, you might just decline his request.

It's not meanness on your part. Not at all. Meanness would be out of character for you. The truth is you're thinking of him. You've got his best interests at heart. And anyway, the rule is that if you can't give a good recommendation, give no recommendation at all. No one would blame you. After all, your opinion has weight now and you need to use that opinion with care. Everybody appreciates that.

But maybe you're not of that opinion. Perhaps you belong to the minority report: you feel that this person has potential. A risk to be sure, but he sought Jesus, didn't he? That's got to count for something! Here in this little meritocracy of ours, initiative still counts. And sure, there are problems, but who doesn't have problems? You? Me? We belong to the First Church of Second Chances, and sometimes third and fourth chances . . . so we agree to write the letter.

Of course, that's the easy part, isn't it? Saying yes is easy compared to putting pen to paper. And even after you've surrounded yourself with glowing superlatives of generous praise, it's not easy. You have to strike a delicate balance. You'd have to be truthful. Not so truthful that his future would be sunk, but sufficiently truthful to live with yourself and any potential trouble down the road, legal or otherwise, if and when things ever went badly as they sometimes do.

Maybe you'd write something like this: "Richie comes from an exceptional family, they're known in the community, lots of buildings dedicated in their name. There's even talk of a brand-new parking lot. And so, naturally, we cannot but think that their son has a lot of potential. He's growing. He's inquisitive. He's searching. He's sincere. Lots of promise, this one, in the right setting, at the right time in his life. He needs someone to encourage him on life's road, a good mentor, a boss who can also be his friend."

Truthful. Fair. Optimistic.

And maybe the disciples would agree with our assessment: under the right conditions, in the right environment, he might make something of himself, might even be fit for the kingdom.

Maybe that's the way we think about Mark's rich man: assessing what the stumbling block was, hedging our bets against his future, trying mightily to be optimistic, and yet always weighing our optimism against his apparent love of money. But something troubles me about this interpretation and maybe it will trouble you too: apparently, between the disciples and the rich man, it seems as if the rich man is the only one who gets it, or at least gets some of it. That is, by the looks of it, he understands better than the disciples the cost of discipleship. He understands better than many, perhaps many in our pews and not a few in our pulpits, the cost of following Jesus.

After all, the rich man of Mark has done something many of us have not done, what the disciples had not done: he has contemplated the cost of following Jesus and found himself wanting. And he was shocked and grieved. By contrast, the disciples, always a little slow in Mark's Gospel, seem to have happily omitted a sober estimation of themselves, what they were prepared to give. Or, if they did make such an estimation, just eking out a "pass" from Jesus, they failed to reflect on the implications of Jesus' way of characterizing his gift to them, namely his life.

According to Mark, Jesus speaks quite openly about this matter, especially in the last three chapters. Plain speech. Telling it like it is. And what does Jesus say? Nothing that we want to hear: he says the Son of Humanity must undergo great suffering, that he will be rejected, that he will be killed, and on the third day rise from the dead.

For their part, the disciples respond by trying to dissuade Jesus, they claim not to understand Jesus, they attempt to massage his plan into something more palatable for popular consumption . . .

By comparison, when the rich man hears Jesus' call, he grieves, for the cost is all too real. His turning away from Jesus in shock and grief expresses greater clarity than the disciple's can boast for themselves: the disciples walk with Jesus too easily, too glibly do they sing his songs, too lightly do they take his name upon their lips.

Truth is, something in the disciples, something in us, something in our humanity refuses to contemplate the cost of discipleship . . . of following the One who says to us, if you would save your life, you must lose it; the first will be last and the last will be first; and to the least of these belong the kingdom.

To such as these, the least, the last, and the lost. And yet, like the disciples we protest: we have labored so long, we have learned so much, we have matured in our faith . . . surely we are worthy, surely the kingdom of God belongs to us as well? Yes, by the grace of God, we can say that it is true. But maybe we forget something about the disciples. Like we sometimes forget about ourselves:

In the beginning, it was God's summons, not our initiative.

It was the word we *heard*, not the word we *spoke*,

It was the bread broken for us

Christ's cup shared between us

the waters of baptism poured out upon us—

Jesus said, "Follow me," and his would-be disciples dropped their nets and left them where they fell. Jesus said to the paralytic, "Rise up, take your mat, and walk." And the lame leaped for joy.

But look at this, friends, look at this because we might just miss it, something crucial for our lives as well as our work. When Jesus looked at the rich man, before he assessed him, before he judged him this way or that, before he said potential here, or trouble there, before he said "gifts this way," or "growing edges that way," before he said he was less or more, good or better, needing improvement or developing nicely . . . before he said any of that, he looked at him and he loved him.

And that, sisters and brothers, changes everything that follows. That love changes everything that comes along in this story. Changes every possible outcome, failure, rejection, success, or even death on a cross.

And if that love is true for the outsider, for the merely curious, do you think it is possible that it is true for those who have been called? True for the disciples? True for you? For us? That God's love gazes on us long before we hear a word of judgment or praise? That God's love gazes on us, pouring the riches of his grace on the deserts of our knowledge? That God's love gazes on us, like the first dawn of an everlasting day?

And if that is true, is it also true for us that as Jesus hung on the cross—is it possible that even as we turned away from him in shock, grief, and horror—is it possible that even then he was turning to us in his redeeming love? That even as we turned from Jesus, that even then he was turning to us in his victorious, resurrecting love?

Is it possible that Jesus' love is the most true thing we should ever know about ourselves, or about the world, or about our neighbor, or about our enemy . . . or about the rejection he suffered, the pain he endured, the cross he died on . . . and the kingdom he inaugurated—if that love is the most true thing, does it not transform everything else?

Our rejections, our denials, our successes, our failures, the gnawing doubt in the dark hour?

Jesus looked at him, and before he said anything, he loved him.

And he loves you.

You have a paper to write, some Greek to translate, a sermon to preach, a prayer to pray. The classroom is only minutes away. It will require much from you. And you, in turn, will require much of yourself. But whatever else you do, do everything in the love with which you are loved—this love, the most true thing we should ever know about ourselves and our world. Amen.

August 2007

7

Learning to Pray in August

THIS IS NOT STRICTLY speaking a confessional sermon, though it, like many of my sermons, employs the genre of personal experience. The biblical texts, which came from the daily lectionary, portions of Job 29–30 and John's account of the death of Lazarus (11:1-16), prompted the topic of the sermon. This is not to say that sermon was not in some deep way personal for me. In fact, these texts haunted me, especially Job 30:20: "I cry to you and you do not answer me; I stand, and you merely look at me."

One can hear the text from Job as a complaint to God and against God. John's story of the death of Lazarus resonates with the bitter complaint of those whose cries have not been heard by God, only this time we hear those cries addressed to Jesus, the Word become flesh. Having noted authorial intent, it is difficult, particularly in view of the church's incarnational witness, to resist the interpretation that these words addressed to God are, at another level, addressed to the church, especially its ministers charged with the responsibility of being present with those who suffer.

When I hear Job's complaint, I sometimes wince at the sharp edge of Job's words. I recall times that, when suffering came, my presence may have been more burden than blessing. I suspect I am not alone. Pastors, too, share this experience, maybe more often than they would like to admit, feeling inadequate to the cry of pain. Sometimes we become jaded to suffering, resigning ourselves to it with cynical familiarity. Suggestive for me in this regard was Thomas's reaction to Jesus' determination to return to Lazarus: "Let us also go, that we may die with him." Thomas's words carry a double meaning. On the one hand, you almost hear Thomas's cynicism, a condition not unknown to those in the ministry; on the other hand, it expresses the truth that, indeed, disciples do follow Jesus to the cross where we meet the One who elected to die with us that we might rise with him.

It bears consideration that our students may be in a very different place than the "seasoned" (or "cynical") pastor. In 2007, the Barna Research Group released a study showing a shift in the explanations for entering ministry given by seminarians under the age of forty. Their study showed that, unlike previous generations who may have described their call in more traditional terms (e.g., pastoring, preaching, Christian education, church administration), today's younger seminarians (under forty years) often cite an experience or perception of pain that led to their decision to pursue ministry.[1]

Anyone who reads through pages of "faith journeys," the essays students write when they apply for admission to seminary, knows this as a matter of fact. One can almost predict what will be found there: divorce, disease, a death in the family, a social crisis like 9/11, among others. Some might bemoan this as the "decline" of the church, lamenting the fact that the church doesn't get the best and the brightest but the most troubled and traumatized. This is debatable, but even if it were true, it seems pretty well irrelevant since they are our students and, indeed, our pastors, not to mention the people in our pews. Fewer people are coming to church (or seminary) because they are "successful," but more and more because they experience themselves as a people in a world of pain.

But if we are indeed witnessing a shift in our understanding of calling, we may need to ask ourselves whether we are helping our future pastors to be more articulate victims or whether we are equipping them with a knowledge of suffering framed within a theological narrative. In that spirit, do our theological traditions give us a way of talking about such experiences? Likewise, does the language of preaching have any ethical obligation to "tell the story" of the voice in pain? And if so, how might it tell that story? Would it in some way be peculiar to the way the church speaks of its life and work in Christ? In other words, by what authority do we speak in ways that are both authentic to experiences of suffering as well as fully expressive of our hope in Christ?

---

1. Burnett, "Social Issues Luring More Young People into Clergy," *Wisconsin State Journal*, May 8, 2007, A1, A9.

"Physical pain," writes Elaine Scarry, "has no voice, but when it at last finds a voice, it begins to tell a story . . ."[2] For the church, our stories are tangled up, even swept up in the life, suffering, death, and resurrection of Jesus Christ—the texts from Job and John seem to "tell the stories" of people in pain, stories that the church needs to hear and speak with redemptive hope.

LEARNING TO PRAY IN AUGUST

I cry to you and you do not answer me; I stand, and you merely look at me. (Job 30:20)

Now a certain man was ill, Lazarus of Bethany, the village of Mary and her sister Martha. Mary was the one who anointed the Lord with perfume and wiped his feet with her hair; her brother Lazarus was ill. So the sisters sent a message to Jesus, "Lord, he whom you love is ill." But when Jesus heard it, he said, "This illness does not lead to death; rather it is for God's glory, so that the Son of God may be glorified through it." Accordingly, though Jesus loved Martha and her sister and Lazarus, after having heard that Lazarus was ill, he stayed two days longer in the place where he was.

Then after this he said to the disciples, "Let us go to Judea again." The disciples said to him, "Rabbi, the Jews were just now trying to stone you, and are you going there again?" Jesus answered, "Are there not twelve hours of daylight? Those who walk during the day do not stumble, because they see the light of this world. But those who walk at night stumble, because the light is not in them." After saying this, he told them, "Our friend Lazarus has fallen asleep, but I am going there to awaken him." The disciples said to him, "Lord, if he has fallen asleep, he will be all right." Jesus, however, had been speaking about his death, but they thought he was referring merely to sleep. Then Jesus told them plainly, "Lazarus is dead. For your sake I am glad that I was not there, so that you may believe. But let us go to him." Thomas, who was called the Twin, said to his fellow disciples, "Let us go also, that we may die with him." (John 11:1–16)

She was given a room on the fourth floor of the Walter Reed Army Medical Center in Washington, D.C., where I was enrolled in a unit of Clinical Pastoral Education. And in June of 1995, when I first met her, the

---

2. Scarry, *The Body in Pain*, 3.

tumor was small and her faith was radiant. In her presence, one felt the earthly presence of a heavenly love.

So, in June, when the tumor was small and hope was radiant,

In June, when I sat beside her for the first time,

In June, on the fourth floor of Walter Reed,

It was easy to pray.

But by mid-July, praying on the fourth floor had become more difficult.

And as prayer grew more difficult,

the tumor seemed to grow more determined.

And by August, she was dying . . . I think she knew she was dying.

And still she hoped, but not like before. It seemed like the kind of hope that has been hurt in its hoping.

I never did learn whether she "won" or "lost" the battle with cancer—my time at Walter Reed had come to an end, and I took my first call. Still, time with her lingered on in my memory. I wondered to myself, that, maybe if I had been wiser, I would have known how to talk with her about the hurt. Perhaps had I been wiser, I would have known how to listen more deeply than I did. What I'm afraid of, however, is that my presence may have only intensified her loneliness, a loneliness echoed in Job's complaint: "I cry to you and you do not answer me; I stand, and you merely look at me."

And I guess, that's the way I imagine Martha and Mary hearing Jesus in the Gospel reading for today. To their cry, Jesus could have said something, anything, other than what we are told he did say: "'This illness does not lead to death; rather it is for God's glory, so that the Son of God may be glorified through it.' *Accordingly*, though Jesus loved Martha and her sister and Lazarus, after hearing that Lazarus was ill, he stayed on two days longer in the place where he was."

Two days too long, it seems.

Martha, I think, summed it up rather charitably: "If you had been here, my brother would not have died." Less charitably, she might have said, "You weren't here, were you? You were off somewhere preaching about glory. And now my brother is dead. Your presence only intensifies my loss. In June there was hope. But it's August now, and my brother is dead."

"I cried to you, and you did not answer . . ."

In June prayer was easy;

    July we can usually endure;

        But August will often haunt us.

It may haunt us because, while suffering is bad enough on its own, that we should pray for redemption and wholeness in a world experiencing unanswerable suffering—to try to answer the "why" question seems almost criminal and perhaps even a form of religious malpractice.

I suspect that the toxicity of the "why" question is in part its stubbornly physical nature.

It is not a conceptual question, which we could happily leave to the philosophers,

    but a physical question,

        standing before us,

            plaintive and righteous in its expectation of answer,

. . . like the young girl's question;

. . . it was a picture in a magazine, I don't remember where I saw it, but she was maybe four or five years old at the most, and it is her question which she asked her mother, her question as they stood behind a refugee fence somewhere in the Sudan, her two little arms ending in the rude stumps that were all the Janjaweed left to her, her question to her mother: "When will my arms grow back again?" She asks the world,

When will I be whole again? When will I play again? When will we hold hands again?

"I cried to you, and you did not answer; I stood before you, and you merely looked at me."

. . . A question full of grief, a physical question that causes voices to shake, and perhaps even the heavens to groan.

Such questions are toxic and are not likely to keep an audience for very long. Even Job's friends, who had presumably gathered around him to support him, spent most of their energy not listening but lecturing. And, looking at the editorial postmortem performed on Job in the forty-second chapter, the portrait of the now-restored, post-9/11, got-back-to-normal Job, it's hardly believable: his lips are too red, cheeks too pink, hair too full, his skin too shiny to be the same man. Perhaps all this is to say that, when confronted with the question of pain, we seem congenitally ill-equipped to listen.

In fact, C. S. Lewis was more honest than many when he declared where pain was concerned, he was a coward: he would crawl through sewage to avoid it.[3] And rumor has it, preachers know the intricacies of the theological sewage system better than anyone else in the world. Unfortunately for us, today's lectionary texts have blocked every practiced escape I can think of. Jesus has turned the prow of faith into the troubled waters of suffering, and we can do nothing but follow where he goes.

So we go, we follow Jesus . . . but we don't have to be cheerful about it. Truth be told, we might even resent him. Thomas is a case in point—he was pretty much resigned to the terminality of August. And I'm inclined to agree with his diagnosis of the situation, considering that . . .

> Having just escaped crowds that would have liked nothing more
>
> than to heave Jesus off the nearest cliff;
>
> Having heard that Lazarus was now irretrievably dead;
>
> Having heard that Mary was probably just this side of hysterics;
>
> that Martha, the steady one, even she was falling apart;
>
> Having heard that they were just entering stage two of the Kübler-Ross
>
> five stages of grief,—you know, the *anger* one—
>
> *Having   heard   all   that,*
>
> Jesus finally decides *now, today,*
>
> is a good time to go to the village of
>
> Bethany.

Jesus is good, very good. But his timing seems a bit off. Wait till September. Things will get better in September. Wait till October; the colors are beautiful that time of year. And by that time, old Lazarus will be pushing up daisies. The anger will have cooled by then, the indignation will have passed. The questions will still be there, true, but at least, they won't be as toxic as they are in August.

---

3. Lewis, *The Problem of Pain*, 93.

But Jesus isn't having it. And Thomas, now resigned to the futility of this journey, says to his fellow disciples, almost under his breath, "Let us go also, that we may die with him."

Something jumps out at me about this comment, about Thomas, and the people he said it to, and it is this: Thomas and the disciples were not casual pew sitters, these were pulpit-pounding, praise-filled, pastoral people, who lived in the presence of Jesus and who, when the tie-mike was safely off, often made light of the pieties in which they could no longer believe.

And maybe that's it: a lack of faith is the problem here. I've heard that sermon so many times, "If you believe, then God . . ." To my ear, such preaching sounds suspiciously like the sermons Job's friends were giving him—and they didn't make the homiletical grade, if you recall. So maybe the problem doesn't fall into the "if you believe, then" formula.

Maybe it's just bad taste on Thomas's part, just one of those instances of graveyard humor, better for the drive to the funeral than the potluck following it, forgettable—nothing more. That could well be, but sometimes I think that sarcasm of this variety is not so much a lack of faith or graveyard humor as much as it is a thin veil covering a felt loss of faith . . . a faith that has been hurt in its hoping.

We had just visited a member of the church who had suffered a stroke and her prospects were not good. By contrast, her husband was with her, gently combing her hair, chattering anxiously about prospects for a recovery that only he seemed to see.

The medical staff did not see hope; neither did the pastoral staff.

As we returned to our car, the minister I was with confessed that he struggled to pray in these situations.

> It seemed useless to him.
>
> What good could it do?
>
> She was going to die.
>
> And her husband was going to resist,
>
> grieve,
>
> and finally walk away from a corpse.
>
> What good could it possibly do to pray?

I judged him harshly at the time, but years later, I discovered that the voice of Thomas grows stronger as the days of August drag on, days that do not give faith, days that grow like a tumor swelling beneath the skin of faith . . .

So, where is the good news here? Perhaps it is not what we would like to hear, at least not at first: we are not immune to August, and what's more, maybe we shouldn't be. Jesus himself wept, his body convulsed with indignation when the full weight of this loss crashed into him. Why should we be any different? Maybe this text gives us permission to be honest about our own hope hurt in its hoping.

Such permission has its place, to be sure. And it is amazing, really, to think about it, but Thomas and Job are still in the church, still beneath this canopy of grace, a canopy that rolls like an ocean, snapping tight with the wind and breath of hallelujahs going heavenward; yes, they're still here, still in the midst of that great cloud of witnesses.

And when Jesus says, "Come, let us go to Bethany," a little farther behind, don't be too surprised if you see the shadow of Thomas, bobbing along behind him, still following, still in the story of his Savior. And Job, well, we still hear him too, groaning from the back pew of faith, still hunched over his grief with an unbearable prayer . . . still there, still in our midst, still in the shelter of the canopy of grace.

Maybe that's the good news, in a strange sort of way: if the likes of Thomas and Job can be included, if they belong in this story of faith, maybe even the likes of you and me belong as well.

But something still nags at me. It's good, of course, to be included, and that's something. But it's not everything. In particular, what I'm struggling with here is all Jesus' talk about this thing being for God's glory, or maybe it's Jesus' peculiar sense of timing. Whatever it is, I'm still left with the feeling that there's more at stake here than just getting by, than just adjusting to a maladjusted world, more than singing a few uplifting hymns on our way to the funeral, more than doing our best in August.

At least one sermon I've heard gives me reason to believe that there is more. As a young seminarian, with a lot of hair and not much else to speak of, I had gone to visit Stan, or rather *The Reverend Stan Anderson*, a man in the advanced stages of brain cancer. I went to pray with him in an August for which I had neither wisdom nor understanding.

But I soon discovered that it was my "lucky day"—I wasn't to be the pastor in this encounter: I was to be a dying preacher's last congregation, his last appointment in a life dedicated to the proclamation of the gospel. And on that August day, he preached from Job.

As he preached, I tried to listen. He spoke about bearing one's cross, persevering through suffering. As he struggled to speak between the shadow of his disease and the glory of the cross to which he testified, Stan gave me something tangible by which to remember his message and the glory of God to which he testified, as boldly in August as he ever did in June. That something is this stole, the one I am wearing today; the one he wore when he celebrated communion on the Lord's Day.

So, you might wonder, after all this, "Do I know how to pray in the month of August?" I don't know. But what I am assured that

When Jesus cries to all the days of the earth and all the tombs of the sea,

>When Jesus says to every tear, *bring forth fruit,*

>To every sigh of surrender, *a shout of victory,*

>To every hurt, *holiness* . . .

On that day, when Jesus says to our Lazarus, "Come out!"

On that day we will see clearly what we now see as through a glass, but dimly. Maybe that's why, when Stan finished his sermon, he celebrated the sacrament. Lifting bread and cup, to receive God's strength, to remember God's presence in August.

Maybe Stan did this so that I would remember. So that *we* would remember, every day, this day, and in all the days of August, the Lord is near:

>More near than the breath we breathe,

>>More near than the fellowship we share,

>>>More near than the tombs that keep us,

>>>>More near than we know . . .

Even so Lord, a Sudanese girl is crying,
 Even so Lord, our Lazarus is dying,
Even so, Lord, even so . . . come quickly. Amen.

September 13, 2006

8

Staying On until Pentecost

People who love the church and its worship sometimes forget its proximity to the classroom, a fact that George M. Marsden points out when he reminds us that "the Reformation began at a university with a scholar's insight..."[1] The classroom may appear dry and musty, its books and those who study them lacking in the stirring eloquence of the pulpit or the dramatic activism of the church and its more public witness, but appearances can be deceptive. A passion for God stirs people to theological study and then keeps them studying; and though study itself seems more likely to give us bad posture than bold proclamation, the truth turns out to be quite different. While I think the best preaching never strays very far from the classroom, chapel preaching owes a special debt of gratitude to the classroom and the scholarship that supports it, particularly since much of the inspiration we experience in chapel has as its primary context the work of a community of students and scholars.

I would say this debt is especially present in this sermon, taken from 1 Corinthians 16:1–9, assigned that day as a part of the daily lectionary. In part, the evidence of that debt shows up when I refer to a somewhat obscure form of Greek grammar, a reference that would be all but lost on any but a seminary audience. However, more broadly, at the time of this sermon, I was leading a seminar focused on preaching from Paul's letters, exploring what appears to be a movement to recover Paul as a vital witness for the churches of today.

Characterizing our contemporary return to Pauline literature as an act of "recovery" may not be a bad way of putting it. According to James

---

1. Marsden, "Soul of the American University," 10.

W. Thompson, homiletical theory of the last decade stressed narrative dimensions of Scripture over and sometimes against nonnarrative dimensions of the biblical witness, which led, in consequence, to an avoidance of Pauline texts: "In a kind of 'Marcionism-in-reverse,' Paul was relegated to the periphery of the preaching canon, reserved for Reformation Sunday, weddings (1 Cor. 13), and funerals (1 Cor. 15)."[2] Some critics claim that narrative theories do not adequately equip pastors to be effective interpreters of Paul's writings.

They may have a point. While the turn to narrative helped pastors tap into the power of story and experience in preaching, we may have unintentionally left the church ill-equipped as interpreters of Paul, a situation that has had disastrous consequences, especially in light of those who continued to use Paul, often interpreting his writings in ways that were detrimental to the marginalized, baptizing a political ideology that had more to do with advancing a narrow social agenda than it did with Paul's cruciform emphasis on Spirit and power. Sadly, the colonization of Paul only contributed to a deepening distrust of his writings among more progressive interpreters. In consequence, we lost a significant voice in the New Testament, a vital theologian as well as a prophetic imagination. When we did hear from Paul, he appeared as a wise quip in the Sunday-morning sermon or, worse, a straw man representing everything mean-spirited and inhuman. We were more likely to apologize for Paul than to be instructed by his thinking on behalf of the church.

This sort of analysis was born out more anecdotally when, after I delivered this sermon, a colleague stated that, almost as a matter of principle, he "never" preached from Paul's letters. Another colleague remarked that she might cite Paul as a supporting text, but usually hewed closely to the narrative texts of the Bible, not feeling confident where Paul's letters were concerned. And to be truthful, I confess that I did not think of Paul as a primary text, at least not very often. When looking at the assigned readings for the day, Paul might have gotten a passing glance as I went eagerly toward a Gospel reading: after all, with the Gospels there is story and Paul, by contrast, offers densely packed argument, more likely to yield interpretive troubles than memorable stories.

That pattern, I think, is fairly common across mainline denominations, but things are changing, and perhaps surprisingly, given the recent

---

2. Thompson, *Preaching Like Paul*, 14–15.

history of Pauline interpretation, we see that change emerging through the provocative scholarship of women like Beverly Roberts Gaventa, in particular her work entitled *Our Mother Saint Paul*.[3] Even in the title, we get the sense this is not the Paul we grew up with but something, or better, *someone* quite different than we imagined. Indeed, imagination appears to be the common link between the narrative movement and Paul, but an imagination cruciform in shape. Gaventa's careful exegetical work with Pauline texts serves the church through scholarship, potentially igniting reformation worthy of the name. But if, as George Marsden argues, the Reformation was begun by the insight of a scholar, it still remains that scholarship has to find its way out of the library, into the classroom, and ultimately into the larger church—or, if not into the church, then maybe into a chapel service, lasting about twenty minutes, plus or minus a Reformation.

STAYING ON UNTIL PENTECOST

Now concerning the collection for the saints: you should follow the directions I gave to the churches of Galatia. On the first day of every week, each of you is to put aside and save whatever extra you earn, so that collections need not be taken when I come. And when I arrive, I will send any whom you approve with letters to take your gift to Jerusalem. If it seems advisable that I should go also, they will accompany me.

I will visit you after passing through Macedonia—for I intend to pass through Macedonia—and perhaps I will stay with you or even spend the winter, so that you may send me on my way, wherever I go. I do not want to see you now just in passing, for I hope to spend some time with you, if the Lord permits. But I will stay in Ephesus until Pentecost, for a wide door for effective work has opened to me, and there are many adversaries.
(1 Cor. 16:1–9)

Tucked away in the seemingly mundane details of a travel itinerary, Paul lets drop this almost offhand remark reflecting his determination to stay in Ephesus: "But I will stay in Ephesus until Pentecost, for a wide door for effective work has opened to me, *and* there are many adversaries" (1 Cor. 16:9b). This sounds peculiar to my ear. You almost want to ask Paul to repeat what he said, make sure you weren't hearing things. What we

3. Gaventa, *Our Mother Saint Paul*.

expected to hear was something like, "There *would* be a wide door for effective work in Ephesus *were* it not for so many adversaries."

If Paul had written that, I would have probably slept through the pericope as well as through this sermon and you and I could have had a nice little nap. It would have sounded like what we often say around here, between classes, at lunch with colleagues, in the church, as we're murmuring about the way the cards have been stacked against us:

"I'd get more done, but I just don't have the time."

"We could really do something in this church, for the gospel, were it not for the members. You know, they're cradle-to-grave Christians, and they've got their hearts set on the grave."

"Yes, if our circumstances were different, we could do something, something significant, something worthwhile. If only things were different."

More often that we'd like to admit, that's the way we talk and I suspect that it is also the way we believe. We make our life plans, not to mention our plans for ministry, in what might be called the subjunctive mood.

The subjunctive mood. James Allen Hewett's *New Testament Greek: A Beginning and Intermediate Grammar*, a book I spent a fair amount of time with as a seminarian, gives us this compact introduction to the subjunctive mood:

> The subjunctive mood expresses contingency, e.g., "If he *were* you"; a non-realized state, e.g., "May he *finish* the course"; or a possibility, e.g., "You *may comprehend*," as opposed to a reality. . . . One uses the subjunctive mood to express a wish . . . a conditional thought that has a questionable likelihood of being fulfilled . . .[4]

So we often speak and so we often live.

But back to Paul. It would make sense that, under the circumstances, with many adversaries, it would be wiser, certainly more prudent, to speak and maybe even make plans in the subjunctive mood. But where we might expect a subjunctive mood, Paul instead introduces us to a peculiar grammar, one that does not come to our tongues naturally or find a place in our hearing easily. In fact, his grammar derives from the faithfulness of God rather than the "bottom line" of markets and trends, of adversaries and friends, conditions that can drive the language of faith into a lowly huddle of what might have been, could have been, should have been . . .

---

4. Hewett, *New Testament Greek*, 62.

but wasn't. If you and I were to hear Paul today, my guess is that maybe from time to time we'd catch ourselves in midsentence, noticing the way we sometimes let the Lord and the door the Lord opens slip away into a storm of conditionally laden clauses.

Our dean, Dr. Longfield, posted these instructive words from C. S. Lewis outside his study in Severance Hall:

> There are always plenty of rivals to our work. We are always falling in love or quarreling, looking for jobs or fearing to lose them, getting ill and recovering, following public affairs. If we let ourselves, we shall always be waiting for some distraction or other to end before we can really get down to our work. The only people who achieve much are those who want knowledge so badly that they seek it while the conditions are still unfavorable. Favorable conditions never come.[5]

Favorable conditions may never come, probably true; but Pentecost is coming, has come, and will come again.

You see, Paul speaks of remaining in Ephesus until Pentecost, pinning his hopes not on the calendar of human conditions, which are always changing, but, rather, on the calendar of God's salvific plan, which is, you might say, steadfast.

You could say that, for Paul, the Spirit has invaded our world, pursuing us relentlessly, whether we were foul or clean, whether we were wise or stupid, whether we lived well or poorly, whether we were God's adversaries or God's friends, whether the markets and trends were up, or especially if they were down, the Spirit seems to delight in opening unlikely doors. And we might even start with Paul, who, in addition to being a fine scholar, was also a persecutor of the church—so he might know something about opening doors among adversaries . . . but even if Paul doesn't, I am convinced God does.

Maybe we could imagine hearing, somewhere in the mystery of the triune life, the Spirit saying, "I am going to Paul,

When he is rising,

When he is crying,

When he is angrily disputing,

When he pierces me,

---

5. C. S. Lewis, "Learning in War Time."

When he curses me,

    When he loves me,

And when he confesses me,

    When he forgets me,

When he praises me,

    When he struggles against me,

    I am remaining with Paul.

Paul can go to the depths, and I am there.

    Paul can go to the far side of the sea, my right hand will keep him.

Paul can be my *adversary* . . .

    But in the mystery of my love,

        I will be his *advocate*.

Paul can curse, but I will bless.

I will remain, for in Paul, I am going to fling open the floodgates of my promise,

    And there are many adversaries."

Funny thing that, all those adversaries Paul spoke about. We have letters he wrote to those communities, love letters almost, love letters indeed. Intimate expressions of care, longing to be with them as an orphan yearns for his mother, as a lover longs for the beloved. Letters written in a bold hand not because they were enemies but because they were a family. Letters written in a wise hand, because he knew time was short and the journey was long and often difficult. Letters spoken in a voice steeped with prayer, prayers for one's enemies, prayers like the Spirit prays, sighing on our behalf, before we knew . . .

Before we knew,

    We were friends.

Corinth, Galatia, Rome, Philippi, Thessalonica, Ephesus . . .
Dubuque, Nenana, Prague, the Sudan, Iquitos, Lebananon, Pine Ridge . . .

Pentecost is coming.

Pentecost is here.

Pentecost is coming.

Perhaps it is winter now, in your life, you may be feeling old, your pastures less rich, your stride slower, your laughter more brittle, your moments of pleasure more fleeting, friends seem few, but of enemies there seem to be many. The days grow shorter, darkness is growing, conditions are against you, the prevailing winds of time and place, they may carry a bitter chill, even so, may we find the courage to say, the confidence to say, "We will remain until Pentecost."

The apostle closes the fifteenth chapter of 1 Corinthians with a victory song. "Death," sings Paul, "has been swallowed up in victory. Where, O Death, is your victory? Where, O Death, is your sting? The sting of death is sin, and the power of sin is the law. But thanks be to God, who gives us victory through our Lord Jesus Christ. Therefore, my beloved, be steadfast, immovable, always excelling in the work of the Lord, because you know that in the Lord your labor is not in vain."

By God's grace, let it be so with us. Amen.

October 22, 2009

9

Nothing, Nada, Zip!

While the Presbyterian Church (USA) is home to me now, I originally came from a part of the Baptist church that was suspicious of the value of education and ambivalent about the role of eloquence in preaching. With that in mind, I have two prominent memories that come back to me when I read Paul's letter to the Corinthians where he declares what sounds like a dogmatic allegiance to ignorance. The first memory is of my return to my home church, where I was baptized, after having been away for a year at seminary. One of the deacons of the church cornered me; he was a severe person and a former Marine, something we were reminded of every time we saw him because he wore a black patch over one eye, probably from a wound suffered in the Korean War.

I remember him setting his hand on my shoulder, drawing me to one side, near a wall, where I felt trapped. "So," he began, "you've been learning some things at seminary?"

"Yes," I said, not used to such intimate conversation between myself and this particular leader of the church. Feeling uncomfortable, I tried to tell him a little of what I was learning at seminary and he listened patiently, though I could tell that he was not especially interested in being instructed by me. His intent became clear when, with the Bible cradled in one hand, he answered my intellectual saga with this memorable observation: "Rob, I want you to know there are a lot of books in the world, but this is the only book that *really* counts. You remember that, okay?"

"Yes, I will," I answered, not knowing quite what I saying yes to but hoping nevertheless a quick surrender could wiggle me out of the corner I felt closing in on me.

The other memory is that of my grandmother, after hearing me deliver a sermon in which I had labored over the language perhaps a little too much. After the service, she gathered my hands into her hands, and quoted the apostle Paul, when he declared that he "came not with eloquence" but proclaiming the folly of the cross.

As I look back on these two encounters, I feel two things, one of those feelings being a sense of frustration: Why should it be that faith in God should narrow the world and not open us up to it? It seems contradictory to proclaim the God contained in the pages of Scripture with the narrow, suspicious, and furrowed brows of thoughtless dogmatism. Sad to say, some students, on entering seminary, cross their arms, narrow their eyes, furrow their brows, and dig their heels into determined positions of dogmatism that have little to do with truth and much more to do with misplaced suspicion of theological education and educators. Most, by God's grace, are not this way; otherwise I think I would find other work. But there are enough of them out there to know that my experience is not isolated.

At the same time, I cannot help but respect and, in fact, be grateful to the church of my youth that gave me the sense to look for the heart of the matter, to never settle for the derivative of faith rather than the font of salvation itself. Our lives are mixed legacies, to be sure, and mine is no different. The sermon below is something of a reflection on that legacy, for better or for worse, but *not* for nothing.

NOTHING, NADA, ZIP!

When I came to you, brothers and sisters, I did not come proclaiming the mystery of God to you in lofty words or wisdom. For I decided to know nothing among you except Jesus Christ, and him crucified. And I came to you in weakness and in fear and in much trembling. My speech and my proclamation were not with plausible words of wisdom, but with a demonstration of the Spirit and power, so that your faith might rest not on human wisdom but on the power of God. (1 Cor. 2:1–5)

"I, Paul—a Hebrew of Hebrews, as for the gospel, I have worked harder than any of them, first among the zealots, as to worldly affairs, a Roman citizen, familiar with the courts, exceedingly capable in disputes religious and secular—I, Paul have decided, determined, resolved . . . to know nothing—'nothing of lofty wisdom,' 'nothing of eloquence,' not even 'plausible words of wisdom'—nothing except Jesus Christ and him crucified."

I want to concentrate this morning on the substance of nothing . . .

The substance of nothing, I have learned, is complicated. That means today's sermon is going to take at least the next hour.

Nothing is complicated. For example, when I ask a significant other, "What are you thinking about, dear?" and the reply is, "Nothing," I know there's something.

It's usually an oversight sort of nothing . . . yesterday, when I left home, I said goodbye to Rebecca and, just before I got into the car, I noticed her at the window with Gwendoline, our three-year-old, who was in the midst of meltdown. Rebecca motioned me to come back inside. I'd forgotten to give Gwendoline a hug and kiss goodbye.

Oh, it was nothing really, unimportant, insignificant, a minor oversight . . . but for her that nothing was a traumatizing something.

Another kind of nothing experience . . . it comes in the form of a dream. It's a dream about preaching. It's formulaic: I have a preaching date, sometimes a location, most often I don't know precisely where the church is at, but I'll get around to it, I'm sure.

As for the text for the sermon: well, I haven't settled on one yet. First it's from the lectionary, and the lectionary frightens me, so then I jump into more familiar arms, but then I forget where it was, what it was, why it was. . . .

Next thing I know, in my dream, it's Sunday, and I'm looking at a congregation who hoped for something and it seems as if all I've got is a pretty certain sense of nothing.

And I came to you in weakness and in fear and in much trembling . . . knowing nothing.

The way Paul speaks of his calling seems somewhat like the way I often speak of my anxiety dreams. Anxiety dreams about the encroachment of nothing, which seems like a rather large something—something that I labor mightily to avoid in places like this one.

I avoid nothing. I acquire something, word by precious word.

You're not so different, hunched over texts, reading your books, writing your papers, saying your prayers, practicing your steps . . . scripted and practiced steps by which you repeat again and again the idea that the world is whole, the cosmos complete, what is up is up and what is down is down.

Our practices, rising up early in the morning, laboring over our books, writing our papers, saying our prayers, each of them reflect our hope that the universe is not slack-jawed and broken. We say to ourselves, the dance floor of life, the theater of our hearts, is as it ought to be: everything in its place, everything for its time.

And I think it needs to be said, that when Paul spoke to the Corinthians, he was not making light of their love of eloquence or wisdom—that is, while on the surface it seems as if Paul is saying these things are nothing, we know that in fact, in his own testimony, they are something to him. And as people who spend a fair amount of time agonizing over the "just right word," we can only imagine Paul similarly absorbed with cadence, pitch, and yes, even, eloquence.

Paul wasn't shy, after all, about boasting, reminding his listeners of his work for the gospel, his fight for the good news. Clearly, Paul is not baptizing Christian ignorance as a virtue. He is not telling us to fling ourselves off the cliff of faith and trust that God will save our precious toes from being banged against the treacherous rocks of reality. Instead, he seems to be saying something much more subtle and profound. And what he is saying is asymmetrical in nature. We get a sharp whiff of what he means when Paul says, "Compared to the surpassing knowledge of Christ Jesus my Lord, I count my gains as loss, and worse than loss." We are familiar with this text. But here he says, "I have decided to know nothing but Jesus Christ, and him crucified."

St. Augustine, preaching from this text says, roughly, "If that is all [Paul] knows then he knows everything."[1]

If that is all he knows, then Paul knows everything.

St. Augustine points to a subtle logic behind Paul's rhetorical gesture here and elsewhere, which is actually more about God and less about Paul:

---

1. ". . . If that was the only thing [Paul] knew, there was nothing he didn't know." From Augustine, *Sermons on the New Testament*, 130.

God who is all and in all,

God who knows all things

becomes,

in Jesus Christ and him crucified,

God's glory veiled in our shame.

God's power veiled in our weakness.

God's wisdom veiled in the foolishness of what we proclaim.

But it is not only God's veiling . . . but it is God's unveiling . . . God's unveiling of our reality. In Jesus Christ and him crucified, we see ourselves unveiled . . . we see ourselves for what we are and not what we should like ourselves to be.

All the words, the practice, the scholarship—for all that they are and they are something—they are passing away. In the hymn "Immortal, Invisible, God Only Wise," we sing, "We blossom and flourish like leaves on a tree then whither and perish, but naught changeth thee."

I read somewhere that Karl Barth kept in his study a print of Matthias Grünewald's *The Crucifixion*, a picture of the dead Christ, skin bursting with sores. Originally it was designed for a hospice reserved for those in the advanced stages of syphilis. People who had, for the world, become as nothing: the not sought, the not called, the not remembered. Barth, this man of many words, to the tune of ten thousand or so pages, kept this picture of Jesus Christ and him crucified, a painting given to people who were not sought, not called, not remembered—he kept this painting nearby. And this is the same man who, when asked by a *New York Times* reporter to name the greatest theological truth of all time, this is the same man who answered with a children's song, "Jesus loves me, this I know, for the Bible tells me so."

The story of the cross reminds the church that we are not nothing in God's sight, but a precious something, daughters and sons, brothers and sisters, named in God's love, remembered in God's promise, saved by God's grace. The cross reminds us that God's love is an electing love, a summoning love, summoning us out of the nothingness of our loneliness and namelessness and forgetfulness into the joyful mystery of fellowship with Father, Son, and Holy Spirit.

God, in Jesus Christ, became nothing so that, by his grace, we could become the new thing of God, fashioned as new people, even as we speak, we become new, created out of the dusts of transgression, the bitter stones of hostility, and the loneliness of our alienation into the singing, praying, preaching, dancing people of God. And the dance floor . . . and the dance floor that seems to be dissolving all around us? It's only getting wider, richer, deeper, with each fearful, trembling, stumbling, grace-filled step into God's future . . . a future unscripted by us even as it is prepared by God.

And our future? Paul says we can't imagine it: "No eye hath seen nor heart conceived what God hath prepared for those who love him."

But maybe Paul wouldn't mind too much, if we took a little sneak peak today, as we celebrate communion, shuffling forward into God's future,

some steady,

    some stammering,

some leaping,

    some weeping,

some praising,

    some wondering,

some praying,

    some quietly thinking . . .

But everyone someone: someone remembered, someone summoned, someone called, someone who was even as nothing now named beloved: cherished son, precious daughter, strong sister, compassionate brother . . . named, saved, and remembered . . . even to the surpassing glory of God. May it be so for us today. Amen.

February 13, 2008

10

Working with Clay

Only infrequently do seminary professors get the opportunity to preach on one of the so-called high days of the Christian year. The following sermon, delivered to the United Presbyterian Church of Miles, Iowa (about an hour south of Dubuque), represents one of those rarities: a seminary professor's Easter sermon! This particular opportunity came about as I was serving the church through pulpit supply as they searched for a new pastor. For me, returning to the local congregation entails a bit of a shift from the by-now-familiar metaphors and rhythms of seminary life, to preaching that becomes quite specific as it attempts to interpret ordinary life with the gospel. Sermons in these contexts must speak a word to people who negotiate the particularities of their work and homes, contexts that sometimes betray no obvious relationship to the church or gospel.

    I will confess that I wonder whether I have made the "right" diagnosis of the local situation; I often feel as though I am preaching in the blind, having become something of a "weekend warrior" in the pulpit. On the other hand, seminary professors do not arrive at an institution of theological education entirely bereft of a congregational background. Seminary faculties come from deep within the life and mission of the local church. Perhaps that is what enlivens chapel preaching most of all, a sense of "home" within the church, that in that place we learned our first language as a community of faith. Nevertheless, that knowledge can never substitute for the deep, weekly rhythms of pastoral life, without which preaching would sound like an empty gong or clanging cymbals.

The sermon below draws heavily from memories of my stepfather, particularly my memory of his hands. It also draws on some of my mother's art, which I mention at the end of the sermon. While my father's hands worked, my mother's hands gave a sense of artistic spirit to an often difficult life—these two images helped me interpret Mark's account of the resurrection, which brings our dutiful, sometimes grim selves into a startling event of dramatic opening to the future.

WORKING WITH CLAY

When the sabbath was over, Mary Magdalene, and Mary the mother of James, and Salome bought spices, so that they might go and anoint him. And very early on the first day of the week, when the sun had risen, they went to the tomb. They had been saying to one another, "Who will roll away the stone for us from the entrance to the tomb?" When they looked up, they saw that the stone, which was very large, had already been rolled back. As they entered the tomb, they saw a young man, dressed in a white robe, sitting on the right side; and they were alarmed. But he said to them, "Do not be alarmed; you are looking for Jesus of Nazareth, who was crucified. He has been raised; he is not here. Look, there is the place they laid him. But go, tell his disciples and Peter that he is going ahead of you to Galilee; there you will see him, just as he told you." So they went out and fled from the tomb, for terror and amazement had seized them; and they said nothing to anyone, for they were afraid. (Mark 16:1–8)

As a boy, I remember looking at my dad's hands with something approaching awe. His hands were like leather, like the leather toolbelt he wore around his waist. Thick, calloused, often with a fingernail blackened by a stray blow from his hammer, his hands looked more like something from the earth than something from the womb; they looked like the gnarled roots of a tree, toughened for work with hard, unyielding earth.

I admired those hands. Those were my dad's hands, as well as my grandfather's, both of them in the same line of work, the construction business.

These were their hands, and I admired them, but I wonder if the same sort of thing can happen, rather more tragically, to our hearts. That is, whatever line of work we are in, whether it is in the office, kitchen, or in the field, our work can be rather like digging into the dirt of life, breaking it open, pulling out of clay whatever life we can find there.

And if it's our whole life, and for many of us it can seem that way, I wonder if our hearts might come to look and feel more like the clay we work with than the hearts we were born with; more hardened by the reality in which we work for our living than tender with the love that first welcomed us in our mothers' arms; more familiar with the tomb than the womb; more defined by the night that will swallow us than the dawn that will awaken us.

Is it possible that our hearts can become so deeply buried in the works of clay—of markets and meetings, of payments and mortgages, of debts and duties—that we no longer feel as if we have a heart at all? That our life is nothing but clay?

That's the look of it as we open our Bible to the sixteenth chapter of Mark. Mark tells us that it was very early on the first day of the week. It was Sunday. But back then, Sunday was their Monday. It wasn't until the fourth century that Sunday became a Sabbath day, a day of rest. When the women get up early in the morning, when the sun is rising, it's a Monday morning—the day that most of us return to the work of clay.

And we see them with their bags of oil and spice, oil and spice to disguise the smell of death. We see them, or rather we hear them, asking each other, "Who will roll away the stone for us, from the entrance of the tomb?"

Like many of us, we come to church looking for something, we are not quite sure what. But what we are sure of are the many obstacles that we face. And those cares can crowd our vision, until all we see are the cares and troubles of this world.

We may ask such questions of ourselves, or of our spouses, questions that are heavy with care, questions like, "How are we going to make it through this month? Never mind retirement, never mind health insurance, how are we going to make it?"

Or, "I don't see how we're going to give our kids a chance to go to college—it just doesn't seem possible."

"Even if I get better, what kind of quality of life am I going to have? Who is going to look after me when I am old? Will I be burden to those I love?"

Or it's an addiction, "I have failed so many times, I've lost count. Why try again? I know I can't do it myself, but I don't know who could help me either."

Most of the time, we don't say such things out loud, except maybe at the dinner table, or perhaps on our way out of the house, parting words to an equally worried spouse. Around here, particularly in church, we put on a brave face, most of the time keeping these fears to ourselves, but the brave face often conceals an even deeper fear, that the obstacles surrounding us will ultimately overwhelm us, that the challenges we face will eventually bury us, that the earth we dig in is actually the grave we will finally sleep in.

Whether we say so or not, it seems to me that's how many of us come to the church, looking for something, we are not quite sure what. What we are sure of is that our feet are heavy with responsibility and our vision crowded with cares. We're looking for something, though we are perhaps not sure of what that something is.

Like the women who went to Jesus' tomb, perhaps we come here looking down, absorbed with the work of clay, wondering how we are going to make it. We look at our hands, gnarled into claws of labor, and unfamiliar with gentle love, and we know we're not getting any younger.

And so we perhaps come. And so they went. Looking down.

But then it happens.

It happens, maybe the way a father or a mother gets down on bended knee before a hurting child, whose eyes are downcast, whose face is hidden in the shadows but whose tears we know: we get down on our knees, we look for their eyes, and with our eyes, not with our mouth, but with our eyes, we say, "Look up, little one, look up."

And faces that hung low now lift, and eyes meet, and we know we are not alone.

The women believed they were alone and they spoke openly about their fears. But Mark tells us, just as they were asking these questions, they looked up, and they saw a sight that took them out of themselves, triggering something like new sight.

In fact, the Greek here is reminiscent of a word Mark uses to describe the blind receiving their sight through the healing touch of Christ.

Perhaps what Mark is telling us is that when the women looked up, they were receiving a gift from the God who looked down, and then came down to our level, even the level of earth itself, living our life, dying our death, and in his resurrection, promising to roll away the stone that threatened to bury us forever.

And as God in Christ bent down to our level, we began to look up to God's level, and when we look in that direction, we are met with the steady gaze of God's love. And in that gaze, looking up, mountains of fear are swallowed up in an ocean of God's grace and power.

So perhaps that's one part of the good news of the gospel for today: God in Jesus Christ says to us by coming down to us, even to the point of death, "Look up, little one, look up!"

But there's something else here as well. We get something that amounts to a second imperative, something like, "Look again!"

I say we are invited to "look again" because the women have already seen where the body of Jesus was laid. Chapter 15 closes by telling us that the women watched where they laid Jesus' body. They didn't need the angelic figure to tell them to look and see where he was laid. Mark already told us that they saw where Jesus was laid. They knew all that, they saw all that, but nevertheless, the Lord says to them through this angelic figure, "Look again."

Why? Why look again? It's rather subtle, something that we lose in translation from the Greek, but according to biblical scholars, when the angel says, "You are looking for Jesus of Nazareth," the word *look* has within it the sense of ownership or possession.

The nearest I can get to it in our own way of speaking is to say, "Have you seen my keys?" Or, "I'm looking for my wallet." It is searching that is focused by a sense of ownership, a sense of property rights. My searching is validated in large part because I have a right to the thing in question.

Telling in this regard is that the angelic figure says, "You are looking for Jesus of Nazareth." He doesn't speak of the Christ, but the man of Nazareth. The women saw the Nazarene body wrapped in linen. Since the body was a Nazarene body, it belonged to them. They had a right to it, after all, the body was only a little bit removed from clay, just as they were, just as we are: entitled to clay.

But the angelic figure says, "Look again, he who was crucified has been raised; look again, there is the place where they laid him."

Perhaps this is the second feature of good news in today's text. Most often, you and I look or search for things that we have some claim on, we look for whatever we are entitled to, and often what we claim seems very small in the big picture. But God is bigger than our entitlement; God is bigger than our property rights. So God says to us, "Look again."

Something like this happened to me the other day, walking with Gwendoline at the arboretum in Dubuque. Walking along a path that bordered a small pond, I found myself "looking again" at something that I hadn't given a second thought: the path we were walking on. It's a well-kept path and it was made for my feet. I know exactly where to step, where the borders of the path are. There's no mistaking it for anything other than a path meant for the exclusive use of my feet. As such, it's not terribly interesting. The pond is interesting, so are the goldfish, the ducks, the flowers that line the banks—all interesting, all things I look at, but the path, I don't give it a second thought.

And so I was a bit surprised when I heard Gwendoline cry out from behind me, "Look, Daddy, look, come see what I've found!" I looked and from where I was standing I couldn't see anything, just Gwendoline on her hands and knees, her nose a few inches above this path that was obviously marked for my feet. So I walked back, got down close to where she was and looked again . . . and sure enough there was a little tiny sprig of something green coming out of that path that I imagined was meant just for me.

Maybe there's something of that in all of life. We say, "It's my life. And I'm going to live it the way I want to." But if Christ is in our lives, and I believe he is, then, as Paul says, we're not only saved, we're *being* saved. Which means our lives are changing, our world is changing; what we took for reality is changing because we are being saved.

I guess it means that all of us, being things of clay, even when we do know God, sometimes we revert to the ways of clay, looking for what is ours, seeing only what we expect to see.

God says, "Look again, and you might just be surprised by the change that I am making in your world."

Look up, your Redeemer is on high.

Look again, there's more to God and God's work in your life than you imagined.

And last, but not least, "Look ahead!"

The angelic figure says to the women, "He is not here, but has gone ahead of you to Galilee; there you will see him, just as he told you."

We are told, last of all, that Christ is not in the grave, but in the world, in fellowship with disciples, maybe even rejoicing in the Spirit.

So look ahead, to a city called Galilee, a place called Miles, to a heart like yours and like mine.

My dad and grandfather both had hands that reflected the nature of their work. But their songs reflected the nature of their faith, a faith that had its seat in their hearts.

How do I know? A lot of things, I suppose. But perhaps the clearest symptom of love in this often difficult world was their voices. You see, they sang in church. Grandpa even sang in the choir. True, they weren't as skilled with their voices as they were with their hands, but I remember listening to them sing the tender songs of God's love, hymnal cradled in calloused hands, making sounds that quieted small children. I knew from their singing that God in Christ was not in some distant place, but instead had come to live in our hearts, even as our hands worked with clay.

In my office, is a clay vase, made by my mother after Rebecca became pregnant with Imogen, our second daughter.

The vase is shaped in the form of a woman's body, belly swollen with new life as well as the labor of life. It was fired in an open pit, so that the clay is a deep gray, scarred with ash. And that's all you see at first: not a woman with child, but a pillar of ash. But as you continue to look at it, you begin to see the belly, the lower back slightly bent, balancing the weight of the child. And then, slowly, something else begins to emerge: you begin to see that the artist has painted the body of the woman with figures, linking hands, and dancing with the song of life, a song that encircles all the ash and all the trouble with the joy of life, with the love of life.

Perhaps that is what it means when the labor of the tomb bursts out with the song of life: yes, there is the work of clay, yes, there is ash, but even more, there is rejoicing, there is celebration, there is hope.

Christ is risen!

He is risen indeed. Amen.

United Presbyterian Church
Miles, Iowa
Easter Sunday, 2009

PART THREE

SENDING

I

A full colonel in the army told me that the single most helpful thing that was said to him in seminary was that seminary is like basic training in the infantry, the purpose of which is to teach you enough to keep you alive long enough so that you can really learn something.[1]

A CRUCIAL EVENT IN my life took place in a trench, around three o'clock in the morning, somewhere on the grounds of Fort Knox, in Louisville, Kentucky, home to America's armor division. I no longer remember exactly the point of the training exercise—training for war, in other words, moral chaos, seems a contradiction in terms—but I do recall the clear sense that if this were to happen we would all be doomed. Specifically, we were instructed to crawl on our bellies across a field, with our M-16s held close to our chests, negotiate barbed wire (crawl beneath it without getting hung up or otherwise injured by it), and then to hold dead still whenever a flare went up into the night sky, bathing our skin in a grey hue. All the while, live machine-gun fire burst over our heads, simulated grenades exploded around us, and tracers raced above us, screaming like angry spears. All told, the experience was less training

---

1. Hoge and Wenger, *Pastors in Transition*, 171.

than an approximation of chaos, something our drill sergeants, many of whom having seen battle with their own eyes, knew to be the reality of armed conflict.

Another crucial event occurred not in a trench, but in an army barracks. At the end of our first day of ROTC basic training, our drill sergeant ordered us onto our bunks, telling us to lie down and cross our arms over our chests, and there to remain, neither speaking nor moving, like corpses staring at the ceiling.

And then the lights went out.

Perhaps our drill sergeant missed the point of military training. According to the citation introducing this section, our military training was supposed to "keep us alive," at least for a while. And indeed, that may well be the point of such training, at least in the books and manuals published by the Department of Defense: survive long enough to learn something, survive long enough to be useful, if not to your mother or your children or your tribe, then at least to your nation. By contrast, it seems our sergeant was dabbling in something far deeper and more dangerous than merely surviving, something like teaching us our death.

Death, it appears, was his art, or his demon, and we, the soldiers assigned to his charge, were his precious medium, medium of blood, skin, and bone—flesh of his flesh, bone of his bone.

Ultimately, I think the colonel mentioned above is wrong—of this I am quite certain. Theological education cannot be reduced to the art of survival, though we do our best to equip students to be faithful and effective pastors to congregations. Despite the way we often live our lives, theological education nevertheless bathes in the waters of baptism, its memory and its work guided by the confidence of God's presence and not by the desperation characteristic of survival. But I am not so sure about the drill sergeant; he seems peculiar to me, his art neither so deceitful nor as common as that of the modern military machine.

Something in him, some memory perhaps, he wanted to tell us the truth . . . tell us the truth with our bodies.

II

"The real exile of Israel in Egypt was that they had learned to endure it."
—Rabbi Hanokh[2]

There may not be an assault course to be found on today's seminary campus (I hope not, anyway), but the "art of war" manifests itself with some regularity, sometimes among students who occupy religious and cultural ghettoes for which they are willing to kill, or between faculty, administrators, and the ideological divisions that separate us. The climate of seminary can sometimes resemble more a battlefield than a community of learning. Of course, to be fair, this looks a bit like the church, squaring off over one issue after another, slaughtering sisters and brothers with as many rhetorical salvos as possible. And we call it "survival," or sometimes, when feeling optimistic, "persuasion."

It would be better, or at least more honest, were we to call it death, our death. Or the symptoms of our death . . .

The symptoms of our dying abound. Today's ecclesiological air swarms with the sound of anxious worry: downward trends in biblical literacy; the eroding influence of the mainline traditions; economic crisis threatening to shutter long-standing seminaries across the country; generalized denominational contraction; the mainline church's shedding of members by the millions; schism constantly in the works; the continuing collapse of mission giving; uncertainty about the church's identity, much less its future; and, not least, the inability of churches to support a full-time pastor.

And what of the work of theological education that we have known through the seminary? Does it make sense to mortgage a home, uproot a family, discontinue health benefits to go to seminary when, realistically, the church, denominationally and locally, cannot pay or even help defray those costs?

And what might we say about distance education, the advent of which is supposed to address the thorny economic questions raised by residential education? While we may gain something in terms of convenience as well as open up theological education to a different kind of student, what are we losing, if anything, that only a residential program

---

2. Buber, *Tales of the Hasidim*, 315.

can provide? What kinds of formative dynamics go by the wayside in an educational setting mediated by a screen rather than a classroom?

And not insignificantly, what becomes of theological educators, many of whom began their vocations as ministers serving real (not virtual) congregations? Will our contact with students be increasingly limited to the screen rather than celebrated at a common table? And how well are we equipped, those of us packing around PhDs, to teach in a virtual classroom, where we are told by the "techies" that gone are the days of the "sage on the stage" and now we are but "guides on the side"? Where does this paradigm shift leave scholarship, the place of prolonged study? And what of the Master of Divinity degree, where does it belong? Is it a relic of the past? With the population of non-ordination-track students growing more rapidly than any other student group, are the learning goals and pedagogical assumptions of theological educators still tenable?

And what of the public witness of the church? As it becomes more obvious that we live in a state of exile, in Babylon, who or what is the church supposed to be? Can we worship Sunday after Sunday, American flag blithely flying in sanctuaries across the United States, as if we did not know that our government tortured human beings, violating the letter and spirit of international law, a law for which American soldiers fought and died? Can we go on as if we did not know that our government deports so-called "illegals," tearing mothers and fathers from their citizen children, rendering those children wards of the state, while at the same time, without even the faintest sign of blushing, we continue to sing the praise of American family values on Sunday morning? When does the incongruity between the God we worship and the state we live in become unbearable?

When do we say it is time to begin a quiet secession from our convenient collaboration with Babylon? When do we say that American Christianity is dead? To borrow language coined by Wendell Berry, When do we begin to practice resurrection?[3]

---

3. Berry, "Manifesto," 275.

III

"... The nation's hoop is broken and scattered. There is no center any longer, and the sacred tree is dead"
—Black Elk (1863–1950)[4]

"Things fall apart; the center cannot hold"
—William Butler Yeats, "The Second Coming" (1919)[5]

When I look at a chapel filling with seminary students, I wonder about the world they are going to, the church they are seeking, the communities that will receive them; maybe most crucially, I wonder about the world they imagine. As soon as a student steps onto the seminary campus, they cast their vision down the years, perhaps imagining the decades of life they have yet to live. But to see the future, we often look to the past and present, at pastors we know, professors in their classrooms, institutions and regularities, all acting like indices of stability, of a universe whose parts operate predictably, mechanically, or at least holistically.

And most of us, professors, pastors, and institutions, do our best to live up to the futures we cannot see. In the circles I walk in, we do not pretend that the crises facing the church are imagined. And yet, in face of those realities, we also know that the church and the narratives we belong to are larger than we are, at least we know this by the light of day. So when we speak of the crises of the contemporary church and its institutions of theological education, we speak of "concerns" rather than "worries," believing that somehow "worry" communicates a lack of faith, all the while covering the early morning hours when we cannot sleep, our minds turning restlessly, anxiously, looking for a center that we trusted but now cannot see, cannot hold, cannot remember.

Sometimes it feels as if we are a language without a presence, a word without a referent, a message without the Messenger. So the church sometimes seems, like a body aching for life, but *a body still*.

Deathly still.

---

4. Neihardt, *Black Elk Speaks*, 270.
5. Yeats, "The Second Coming," 91.

And yet it appears just here, in this very stillness, the paradox that we did not seek, the death we did not embrace, the body we could not, dared not imagine.

Stillness where Presence sings and mystery abounds . . .

"Be still, and know that I am God" (Ps. 46:10).

". . . earth . . . a formless void and darkness" (Gen. 1:2a).

". . . but the LORD was not in the fire; and after the fire a sound of sheer silence" (1 Kgs. 19:12b).

To be still, deathly still, like the stone waiting to be struck by the staff of Moses, split for unlikely water, this movement expresses a dynamic rather than static universe, one of dramatic transformation rather than the pretense of static life.

This much, I think, we will happily receive: the concept of stillness before transformation. And even if we are not willing to receive silence, we are nevertheless familiar with the formula: How many times, in a course on spirituality or before a sermon, have we been asked to "empty our minds" as we listen for God's word? Apart from those who are "uncomfortable with silence," many will welcome this posture, perhaps even running to this sort of silence. But why, when we finally finish talking about "spirituality," do we oppose transformation, fleeing from it at all costs? Could it be because we never really sought transformation to begin with? And even more, because that transformation, and the death it implies, terrifies us?

Impressive in this regard are biblical texts that evoke imminent transformation not through our quietude but through something approaching wild terror: "My anguish, my anguish! I writhe in pain! Oh, the walls of my heart! My heart is beating wildly; I cannot keep silent; for I hear the sound of the trumpet, the alarm of war" (Jer. 4:19). Then, the prophet imagines the unmaking of the creation: "I looked on the earth, and lo, it was waste and void; and to the heavens, and they had no light. I looked on the mountains, and lo, they were quaking, and all the hills moved to and fro. I looked, and lo, there was no one at all, all the birds of the air had fled" (Jer. 4:23–25).

Similarly, we might hear Job, the world he knew swept away, as he cries out from the ash heap, desiring to return the creation to darkness: "Let the day perish in which I was born, and the night that said, 'A man-child is conceived.' Let that day be darkness! May God above not seek it, or light shine on it. Let gloom and deep darkness claim it. Let clouds settle upon it; let the blackness of day terrify it. That night—let darkness seize it!" (Job 3:2–6a). Interestingly, Job's outburst was preceded by a kind of silence: "They sat with [Job] on the ground seven days and seven nights, and no one spoke a word to him, for they saw his suffering was very great" (2:13). Perhaps their silence is an ironic one, suggesting more platitude than presence; offering a lament may be the more faithful word amid God's silence. Whatever the nature of the separation Job experienced, the poet breaks into a prose world, interrupting its conventions, and even its "good conventions" with the jagged edge of lament. One could say that Job's word takes us to a place where we would not go—in a manner of speaking, Job's speech "sends" us to a place where we cannot speak, our speech reduced to the cries of a soul writhing in pain and then, in exhaustion or death, to silence.

We do not die easily . . . or at least we do not do so with grace.

We resist and actively develop antidotes to the suffering that comes with dying—not only the death of our bodies, but the agues of the spirit. Mostly, these antidotes mask our sickness unto death without actually changing it, much less transforming it. Jeanette Winterson, a novelist, believes that we risk losing something of ourselves, something of our richness when we surrender the aching lament: "I have never taken antidepressants because I couldn't face the flatness. I preferred the highs and the crashes, even though it meant the rages and withdrawals, and anyway, I'd rather have my own suffering than someone else's solution." More to the point, she worries that we will exchange authentic change for a cheap counterfeit: "Too often, we're sold transformations of the unreal. The life plans, guru weekends, self-help manuals, get rich/thin/happy programs are no different than upgrading the car/house/job/wife/boyfriend ethos that confuses surface activity with change."[6] While we may differ on the relative value of antidepressants, we may nevertheless recognize our own capacity for self-deception, introducing flatness where jagged edges might otherwise exist.

We exchange the sharply angular language of lament for the linear language of solutions. Or perhaps we find our answers to terror in the softly bland manner of some contemporary expressions of spirituality. Or, maybe, as institutional bodies, we look to markets, trends, and revenue

---

6. Winterson, "In Praise of the Crack-Up" (online).

streams, reducing every art to a number, and every person to a dollar amount. Either lacking vision or, more likely, fearing it, we prefer the crisp truths of these figures, offering, as they seem to do, an irrefutable "final solution" for our contemporary troubles. And still, with haunting regularity, we hear Jesus' disruptive cry from the cross: "My God, my God, why hast thou forsaken me?" Despite our desire to comfort that cry of terror, there is, according to Gerhard Forde, no "answer" to this cry: "We can't answer Jesus' question. We can only die *with him* and await God's answer in him."[7]

IV

Entropy, particularly the phenomenon of increasing chaos, strikes me as suggestive in regard to the theology of the cross. Where we often see (or imagine) science and theology parting company, it seems that around the theology of the cross we see a meeting of sorts, namely in the second law of thermodynamics:

> The first law [of thermodynamics] states that all matter and energy in the universe is constant, that it cannot be created or destroyed. Only its form can change but never its essence. The second law, the Entropy Law, states that matter and energy can only be changed in one direction, that is, from usable to unusable, or from available to unavailable, or from ordered to disordered. In essence, the second law says that everything in the entire universe began with structure and value and is irrevocably moving in the direction of random chaos and waste.[8]

Jeremy Rifkin proclaims the entropic principle to be the "supreme physical rule of the universe [that] pervades every facet of our existence."[9] And yet, despite its reach, we nevertheless pretend that, through scientific innovation or an optimistic spirit, we can "get around" the "one-way path from useable to non-usable" resources.[10]

Rifkin compares those who ignore the principle of entropy to "the man who refuses to believe in gravity." He leaps off a high building to demonstrate its nonexistence and, as he falls past the fortieth floor, declares,

---

7. Forde, *On Being a Theologian of the Cross*, 3.
8. Rifkin, *Entropy*, 6.
9. Ibid., 241.
10. Ibid.

"So far, so good."[11] The church seems to enjoy a slight advantage over Rifkin's imaginary optimist: every year, congregations gather together on Ash Wednesday, and speak these sobering "entropic" words: "From ash you have come and to ash you shall return."

So, the church speaks of death, too, reminding us of our end. Yet, at this point, we may need to part company with science, even as we benefit from its clarity. We have a story—a story that, like the Spirit, goes ahead of us. Even the cry of Jesus in Mark's Gospel tells the story of his resurrection, on the breath of his lament, as it evokes the memory of Psalm 22. But the knowledge of the resurrection in no way diminishes the terror of his cry, no more than the "ending" of Job "answers" Job's complaint. Nevertheless, the chaos of crucifixion is carried forward on the breath of faith.

Perhaps that sense of faith lets Paul speak of his death as he does, without apology, without blushing; but he does not speak of it in the despair that we would ordinarily expect. Despair, of course, may not always be as transparent as the despair we hear in lament. Optimists express despair through delusion—they are especially tragic because they never actually address their reality. Sometimes despair appears in the attitude of a pragmatist, who merely "tinkers" with waste and chaos, never introducing any real resistance. A hedonist's decision to "live for the day" expresses despair as well, as it swallows all hope and all imagination, as if there were such a thing as *living* for the day alone. All these attitudes or postures are present in today's churches—and none of them can begin to answer the very real crisis confronting the church today.[12]

Paul, by contrast, speaks differently and, as a consequence, acts in ways that are startlingly contrastive in nature. He *conceives* himself, particularly of his apostleship, using the peculiar grammar of the cross, declaring, "I die every day" (1 Cor. 15:31) and "It is no longer I who live, but it is Christ who lives in me" (Gal. 2:20) and "I carry the marks of Jesus branded on my body" (Gal. 6:17). He proclaims Christ in his body, on his body, clothing his body through the promise of Christ's death and resurrection. We see a paradox, for not only does Paul speak of his *death* but of his *body*, and indeed our *corporate body* in Christ, anticipating Christ's answer. Our bodies groan in anticipation of the Spirit's answer.

11. Ibid., 242.

12. Rifkin's chapter, "From Despair to Hope," in *Entropy* supplied the general categories for this paragraph; see 253–60.

A student, Christie John, when preaching from 1 Thessalonians, described the peculiar character of Christian waiting as *lively anticipation* rather than passive resignation. Paul says to the church at Thessalonica, even though it is dark, "Let us keep awake and be sober" (1 Thess. 5:6) ; "let us encourage one another and build up each other" (v. 11); "rejoice always, pray without ceasing, give thanks in all circumstances" (vv. 16–18a); "test everything; hold fast to what is good; abstain from every evil" (vv. 21–22)—the stones groan with the longing of the Spirit.

This sense of anticipation emerges as a sigh of hope rather than the sigh of despair. Yet, we probably should not lose sight of the sense that Paul's experience of calling was hardly an "easy" translation, from despair into hope. Paul says he came into his calling as "one untimely born," or more literally, "born" as a miscarriage (1 Cor. 15:8). Paul, according to Gaventa, imagines his birth into his work as an apostle using unsettling language.[13] With Paul, we look in vain for the easily accessible hope that comes with conventional ways of talking about calling, that is, from worse to better. Instead, Paul portrays his ancestral birth, a self-evidently good birth (e.g. Phil. 3:4–6), as trumped by his cruciform birth, a birth that seems all too obviously wrong. Paul was conceived in Christ as the "worst"—in the likeness of the cross—so that he might participate more faithfully in the proclamation of Jesus Christ and him crucified.

The presence of the Spirit insinuates itself into the "waste and chaos" of the cross with resurrection promise. Martin Neimöller describes this haunting scene from the Dachau concentration camp: "There was a scaffold in the courtyard of our prison in Dachau concentration camp. I used to look at it every day to receive its sermon. I had to pray a good many times because of it."[14] To speak of "receiv[ing] its sermon" implies that the darkest circumstance has been invaded by a transformative message. Even so, we only apprehend this through faith; never by sight.

Still, as Paul reminds us, "we do not know how to pray as we ought, but that very Spirit intercedes with sighs too deep for words" (Rom. 8:26). Something outside of us, not within us, intercedes on our behalf.

---

13. Gaventa, *Our Mother Saint Paul*, 26.
14. Neimöller, "Grace," quoted in *Against Torture*, 80.

V

Rebecca, my spouse, might characterize her experience of pregnancy, particularly the first trimester, as one long bout of nausea. For her, "morning sickness" is a misnomer; nausea afflicts her morning, afternoon, night, and early morning hours. As we talked to other women who experienced this kind of severe morning sickness during their pregnancies, they spoke of breaking down into uncontrollable tears. One said, "I just cried, it was awful." Mood swings, acute sensitivity to smells, loathing food and yet needing it, eating and yet stricken by bouts of uncontrollable retching—Rebecca tells me that this must be the way it feels to die. I suppose that every pregnancy occasions a kind of death in life, particularly as one learns that the body you inhabit as your own is now making room, apparently unwillingly, for another inhabitant. I read somewhere that the symptoms of pregnancy resemble those experienced by people with a tumor—the rapidly growing fetus invading the once-hallowed, private space of the body. Life and, indeed, change, has an intrusive quality. To recall the biblical Rebekah, experiencing life may lead us to question life itself: "If it is to be this way, why do I live?" (Gen. 25:22).

At about ten weeks or so, Rebecca visited our prenatal care provider to begin what would be monthly visits to check on the progress of the pregnancy, which, for her, really feels just like sickness. But when the nurse placed the stethoscope against her belly, and she heard the confident "swish, swish" of a heartbeat, deep in her womb, she felt as if something new were happening in her, despite the sickness, in some subtle way transforming the sickness she felt in her body to a life she anticipated in her heart's imagination.

"For the first time," she said, "I felt pregnant and not just sick."

Our first faculty meeting in the spring of 2009 opened with the stark realization that theological education as we have known it, as the church has known it, is sick unto death. Administrators use apocalyptic language to describe the economic conditions confronting seminaries across the country. Similar language appears in the church as well, as denominational leaders openly question the viability of contemporary denominations. Today, we get regular updates of the "end" without much sense of the future. Teachers and students return to their classrooms wondering whether the paradigms of education and church will last into the decade. Or, more morosely, they wonder who is going to make it to the "bottom" first. Of course, the truth is that the economic realities of the "Great Recession" are just the most recent, and perhaps not even the most important, symptoms of our condition. Whatever else we may believe, we are witnessing a dramatic implosion of denominational structures and institutions. And, our grief, in church and seminary, is very great indeed.

But there are countervailing symptoms, almost like sighs too deep for words . . .

Not long ago, a group from a regional governing body, made up of pastors and lay leaders, came to visit our seminary. It was strange, this visit, the first of its kind in my memory. Of course, we get the obligatory visits from church executives, moderators, bishops, and distinguished graduates, not to mention those groups we have cultivated as church-based advisors to the seminary community. These visitors sometimes preach in chapel, lead a conversation among students and faculty, have consultative conversations between faculty and the administration, all in an attempt to keep the connection between church and seminary as lively as possible. But this visit felt different, its purpose not explained. We were told they wanted to talk to us, to hear about us, to dialogue with us about the church—and, in honesty, for many of us, this seemed an inscrutable proposal, though it seemed most natural.

On the assigned day, at the assigned hour, we gathered at the designated meeting place, but it was like the eighth-grade dance. We stared at each other awkwardly, the music playing but the dance floor between us as vast and empty as any gym floor from our adolescence, none of us seeming to know the way across our curious estrangement. Slowly but coyly, we began to talk. First introductions, where we were from, what we were doing, how long we had been doing it. But then, deeper questions and more revealing conversation. What, they asked, can we do for you? What in your scholarship will help us to meet the changing needs of the church? These questions, and others like them, were welcome questions for us, questions we were prepared to talk about. For myself, this expression of affection was a welcome, almost dizzying surprise since I had experienced nothing quite like it in the past.

But then, interrupting our excited conversation about the relationship between the seminary and the church, one of the members of the group asked a question to which he seemed to know the answer.

"Do you pray for us?" he asked, a little sad perhaps.

It was not a mean question. He asked this question among other questions, but clearly it was the question that weighed upon his heart. But once the question was in the open, it lingered there, like a bare naked branch jutting out of an otherwise healthy tree. There was some shuffling at the table, fiddling with our coffee cups, embarrassed assurances that, yes, we did pray for the church, but it was a strange question, one we were not used to hearing, not used to recalling.

But there was something else as well. Beyond its awkwardness, it almost seemed to open our ears to something lively between us, unconditioned, insinuated between our mutual houses collapsing.

VI

Whatever becomes of the current structure of the church and its institutions of higher learning, it will not be like the church or classroom we have known, that many of us were shaped by, and that many of us still cherish.

To take but one example, the advent of so-called distance education, a phenomenon that raises all kinds of questions for church and seminary alike. But one of the most important questions, so far as I can tell, is not whether distance education works or not but what role the church and seminary will play in taking the "distance" out of theological education as a whole, whether the classroom takes the form of residential or online study.

In fact, one of the flaws of residential programs is just this: the church sent its prospective ministers "away" to seminary for three years of intensive study. Some would object that at least part of that study takes place in "field placements," or ministry sites where a student receives mentoring from a pastor or other religious professional. This kind of formation often proves crucial in vocational development. Additionally, residential education proves invaluable as it opens students to new possibilities, taking prospective pastoral leaders out of their familiar contexts and exposing them to a range of historical and contemporary interpretation. In a context of the unknown, that is, a seminary classroom, assumptions about the known are inevitably examined, tested, and revised. Moreover, residential models of theological education frequently forge a lasting relationship between student and teacher, cementing a lifelong commitment to learning.

But there is a flip side to this scenario: for most local congregations, theological education presupposed the phenomenon of displacement as their *members* became *seminarians*, as people of the church were socialized into a professional class, sometimes leaving seminary unfamiliar with or embarrassed by the life of the local congregation. Additionally, economic forces are set into motion creating a condition in which seminary-trained pastors cannot serve the kind of community they would prefer, but, under economic duress, must seek out the "highest-paying" communities. Those who "succeed" leave imperiled congregations as soon as reasonably possible. This pattern becomes most pronounced among marginalized communities, where people from these communities go to seminary and often never return.

Of course, we may need to revise our sense of language here, since most churches are, in fact, marginalized communities. But this is only a more recent event for the majority cultures that created the system of theological education we have now. Among Native peoples, the problem of theological education by displacement has a long and complicated history. For example, in a paper entitled "Mending the Hoop," published in 1974, Native church leaders identified a host of problems confronting Native churches. Among these was the sense that residential programs "were causing cultural disruption" to embattled Native communities. How so? Residential education, they argued, trains people who *want* to be leaders rather than, in collaboration with tribal leadership, identifying those who have been *formed* as leaders by their respective communities, the ordinary manner of leadership formation in Native cultures. And even when a community-formed leader is raised up and "sent" to seminary, traditional patterns of theological education work by "extraction" rather than incarnation. Additionally, the costs of residential programs of education further inhibit the development of capable leadership for marginalized churches since, by the end of their course of study, their communities can no longer afford to compensate their leaders, almost guaranteeing that seminary-trained Native leaders will end up serving predominantly white congregations or institutions.[15]

While speaking specifically of Native communities, the writers of this paper are in fact naming a larger crisis that many churches have been sensing for some time: in our uncritical adoption of *distance* education

---

15. "Mending the Hoop: Results of Research by the Indian Church Career Project (Summary)."

(that is, residential education), the church turned over the vitally important work of theological education to what might be seen as an "absentee" classroom. I do not intend to strike an excessively critical tone vis-à-vis residential programs of education; I am a product of this tradition and I cherish much about it. However, it gives me pause that, under the current paradigm of theological education, some of the most decisive years of pastoral formation take place not primarily in the life of a congregation but in the life of a seminary that sometimes struggles to see itself a reflection of the church as a whole or contributing to the leadership base of a particular community.

Another dimension of the drift between classroom and church exists in the postseminary experience of many pastors: the seminary classroom is left behind. Or at least, the vital relationships between practicing pastors and theological educators become more sporadic and less organic. If a pastor elects to do so, she or he may pursue a DMin after three to five years in the pastorate, but what of those intervening years? Recent graduates often receive calls to communities where they enjoy few of the resources common to a seminary community and perhaps none of the familiar comforts they enjoyed in their home church. Perhaps at one time this was a tolerable scenario, but with the church struggling so profoundly, the toll it takes on new pastors and the congregations they serve may be too much.

New pastors are asked to reconcile the incongruities between their present calling and their educational experience with little guidance from either the larger church or the seminary community. While some may negotiate those tensions with greater skill than others, many seem to founder, either staying in their first call for only a few years or, after six years or so, dropping out of ministry altogether.

Now, with online education, that is, "distance education," churches worry whether the kind of formation that previous pastors received will happen for online students. Some of their concerns come out of a sense of pedagogical strategy. For example, these concerns might point to a class like homiletics: How can preaching be taught through distance education? Most online programs of study try to answer this concern with a residential component of education, reserved in particular to classes like homiletics. But the question still has validity, although in a broader context. That is, I suspect our worry about online education belongs elsewhere, especially given that the church has had "distance education" for a long time. A fair question appears when we ask whether some of the more glaring deficiencies of pastoral leadership are not related to the drift between church and classroom—a distance that poses enormous threats to the missional and evangelical enterprise of the church.

However we finally come down on the relative merits of online and residential programs of study, it seems to make sense to begin to reflect on ways in which the church and local communities of faith can begin, in partnership with its teachers, to take a more active, vital, formative role in the classroom, whether residential or online. Similarly, theological educators can no longer think of education and the relationship between student and teacher as a three-year stint of graduate study. The old dispensation of theological education may have worked for its time but it is not working now.

At the same time, we enjoy more common ground than we imagine. Every classroom, even the online classroom, exists in close proximity to the church through chapel, an intersection where church and seminary foster crucially important conversations. Interestingly enough, the so-called distance education students, when they arrive for the residential component of their study, four weeks each year, boast almost 100 percent chapel attendance, something unheard of among residential students. While online education may not be for everyone or an answer to the problems confronting theological education for the church today, we should not dismiss it, or the students who have enrolled in such programs, too quickly. They may be in a position to help the whole church recover its vocation as a classroom of the Spirit.

VII

The sermons that close this collection reflect, I hope, the mystery of the way of the cross, guiding us in a way we would not go, in a way we did not imagine. Sometimes, while preaching, I try to see things in a cruciform light, taking darkness and chaos as the ground of witness. The Spirit sends us into places we cannot know because the Spirit sends us as New People, whether telling stories of inexpressible pain, or the church imagining its body as the body of the desperate poor, or imagining the church cultivating the creative chaos of a community garden, we do so in a spirit of hope. After all, before we were a New People, we were no people at all—just chaos and waste with optimistic names.

We are changed; by God's grace, we are not the same.

In the spring of 1995, on the final day of a seminar with Herman C. Waetjen, professor of New Testament at San Francisco Theological Seminary, he concluded our hour with what struck me as a curious charge. His blue eyes electric and face flush with passion, he flung open his arms, offering a word to keep us, a last word to guide us:

"Embrace the chaos!"

He spoke, as I recall, in the spirit of prayer.

11

Looking for Someone to Blame

When I review this sermon on Hebrews 11:29—12:2, out of the daily lectionary, I question my interpretive judgment, wondering if I am not coming dangerously close to endorsing the violent theology of the cross, a violence that all too often falls on the shoulders of women. That said, I ultimately chose to preach the sermon, despite its troubling turn, in which I recount one woman's experience of rape. Why did I choose to continue with this interpretive course, mindful of my own social location and sympathetic to feminist and womanist critiques of violence in Christian witness? In sum, I would say there are three reasons I continued with it: the biblical text; the theology of the cross; and my evolving view that contemporary expressions of victimhood carry implicit anthropologies that, on closer examination, are inadequate in view of a rigorously theological anthropology.

To begin with, this particular lection offers an unusual cut of this epistle, beginning with the troubling, albeit eloquent, exposition of redemptive suffering in chapter 11 and culminating with the climax that begins chapter 12: "Therefore, since we are surrounded by so great a cloud of witnesses . . ." While I have often cited this text, I had, up to this time, never juxtaposed this almost wispy expression of the witness of the church with the frankly bloody account of martyrdom offered in 11:35–38. Perhaps especially troubling is the intimation of the collapse of the mental and emotional faculties of those who suffered (vv. 37b–38), descriptions that recalled to my mind the accounts of those who suffer post-traumatic stress from experiences of war or torture. Victims often never actually recover, their bodies and minds carrying the marks of violence and terror.

But what gives me pause, even now, is that the writer of Hebrews did not attempt to disguise the shattered humanity that martyrdom left behind. Unlike our own tendency to "make it good" the writer of Hebrews names the havoc wreaked by suffering and then says forthrightly that those who suffered so grievously, "though they were commended for their faith, did not receive what was promised . . . " (v. 39).

Paradoxically, the preacher in Hebrews does not see "through" the suffering of innocents, calling the evil good, but in a flatfooted way declares that we "see" by way of an uncreated light. In the words of Artur Rosman, "God appears to be a creature of the night, hidden when he reveals himself . . ."[1] Rosman's insight, as you might deduce, comes as a staple to the theology of the cross: the witness of the cross invites us to "dim our lights theologically," forcing us to wade into the murky waters of faith.[2] Once the writer of Hebrews had "dimmed" my theological lights, I saw that this "great cloud of witness" was not this wispy cloud of saintly repose that I had so often imagined but, instead, a cloud streaked with crimson and the cries of injustice.

By way of confession, as a preacher and practical theologian, I am not especially at ease with theoretical accounts of atonement. Sally Brown wisely advises us to "avoid *any* single-theory approach to atonement, however well intentioned."[3] Speaking in terms of the actual language of preaching, she stresses the evocative and contextually grounded language of Scripture over the linear language often characteristic of theoretical accounts of atonement: "New Testament cross talk is local, pastoral speech..."[4] Just as significant, being a theologian of the cross in the pulpit, according to Gerhard Forde, leads us to "tell it like it is."[5] That is, one of our tasks as preachers is the act of dismantling the illusions of a theology of glory with the unsparing but crucially redemptive account of the Crucified God.

Still, while I understand the theological commitments that shape my interpretation of this text, I must say that this kind of preaching terrifies me, because its implications are so much greater than my faculties of perception. There is an insoluable mystery here, one that does not dissolve before the acids of theoretical explanation. There is a sense that we

---

1. Rosman, "Acquainted with the Night," 32.
2. Ibid.
3. Brown, *Cross Talk*, 63.
4. Ibid., 27.
5. Forde, *On Being a Theologian of the Cross*, 13.

come to this place in the same way that Richard Lischer says people visit the Holocaust museum or Dachau: "The normative demeanor is silence."[6] And yet, at the same time, as those who are addressed by the promise of the cross and empty tomb, we come with an almost unseemly anticipation for God's speaking. Perhaps it is what Paul means by the "foolishness of what we proclaim," waiting for God's answer, the only answer that can possibly mean anything amidst the unanswerable grief of human suffering. Yet still, even as we listen, the church goes about its quietly courageous act of proclamation, breaking bread and hoisting the cup, proclaiming his death until he comes.

LOOKING FOR SOMEONE TO BLAME

By faith the people passed through the Red Sea as if it were dry land, but when the Egyptians attempted to do so they were drowned. By faith the walls of Jericho fell after they had been encircled for seven days. By faith Rahab the prostitute did not perish with those who were disobedient, because she had received the spies in peace.

And what more should I say? For time would fail me to tell of Gideon, Barak, Samson, Jephthah, of David and Samuel and the prophets—who through faith conquered kingdoms, administered justice, obtained promises, shut the mouths of lions, quenched raging fire, escaped the edge of the sword, won strength out of weakness, became mighty in war, put foreign armies to flight. Women received their dead by resurrection. Others were tortured, refusing to accept release, in order to obtain a better resurrection. Others suffered mocking and flogging, and even chains and imprisonment. They were stoned to death, they were sawn in two, they were killed by the sword; they went about in skins of sheep and goats, destitute, persecuted, tormented—of whom the world was not worthy. They wandered in deserts and mountains, and in caves in the ground.

Yet all these, though they were commended for their faith, did not receive what was promised, since God had provided something better so that they would not, apart from us, be made perfect.

Therefore, since we are surrounded by so great a cloud of witnesses, let us also lay aside every weight and the sin that clings so closely, and let us run with perseverance the race that is set before us, looking to Jesus the pioneer and perfecter of our faith, who for the sake of the joy that was set before him

---

6. Lischer, *End of Words*, 6.

endured the cross, disregarding its shame, and has taken his seat at the right hand of the throne of God. (Hebrews 11:29—12:2)

"By faith the people passed through the Red Sea as if it were dry land..."

It's interesting to hear this first line from today's text in light of the well-known description of faith offered at the beginning of the eleventh chapter: "Faith is the assurance of things hoped for, the conviction of things not seen" (v. 1).

It's the second clause of that sentence, "the *eleng-kos* of things not seen" that caught my attention this week.

The NRSV actually follows Augustine, who sometimes translated *eleng-kos* as "conviction." Calvin, on the other hand, while approving of Augustine's translation, prefers "demonstration," reasoning that it is the more literal expression. Let's just say we hang out with Calvin this morning, choosing literalism as our exegetical partner: "Faith is the assurance of things hoped for and the *demonstration* of things not seen."[7]

So as the people passed into the Red Sea, they could not see or have concrete knowledge that the waters would part, but they walked on "as if it were dry land"—as if the promise of God's deliverance were more real, more *demonstrated* than the waters that lapped against the shoreline in front of them, as if that promise were more urgent than the army rushing up behind them, even more foundational than their hearts that surely beat wildly within them.

As if it were true.

As if the obstacles and resistance to going forward, both within and without, were parting even now, even before we could see it, even before we could push it aside, even before we acted in faith.

As if it were true that God acts, that God delivers, that God works with and through the likes of you and me—and maybe even demonstrates our hoped-for futures through a church that lives, walks, and works in a world where the Red Sea seems only to rise and the feeling, no, the *experience* of persecution seems only to grow.

As if it were true.

As if it were real.

---

7. Calvin, *Commentaries on the Epistle of Paul to the Hebrews*, 228.

Maybe it was something like this that ultimately led Heather Gemmon Wilson and her family to choose to live in the inner city.[8] It didn't start that way. Like most penniless college students, they were sensible people—they moved there only for a time, and out of necessity, and once necessity had expired, they planned to leave for someplace safer, more familiar, more fitting.

But there was a church, a living church, as it happens. Community development was a regular part of their Sunday-morning vocabulary. *Racial reconciliation wasn't politics, it was the gospel.* And she says, "They were hooked"—as if it were real.

Changed their lives. Instead of sitting behind shuttered windows, they sat out on the front porch. The kids who at one time seemed more like menaces than neighbors slowly became their friends, even their adopted children. They began working in the garden together. She says, "The hood became our home." "If it weren't for the church," she says, "I wouldn't have been living in that place four years and two kids later."

The hood became our home . . . a demonstration of things hoped for, and perhaps even things we did not imagine to hope for.

As if it were true.

And she was raped.

Heather says if it weren't for the church, it might not have happened. She would have lived somewhere else, more suburban, more gated, more secure.

If it weren't for the church, a living church as it happens.

Maybe it would have been different for them, too. The writer of Hebrews tells us what happened: tortured, sawn in two, beaten, put in chains, driven into destitution, wandering, and hiding in fear, even to the point that they were living in holes in the ground.

Persecuted, tormented, tortured, maybe (probably) raped.

If it weren't for the church, a living church, it might not have happened.

"Rape," she writes, "is ugliness in its basest form. It destroys innocence and replaces it with shame. It steals a sense of security and extends fear. It cultivates bitterness. It leaves no room for beauty. The overpowering emotions I experienced that awful night did not go away the next day—or the one after that."

8. Adapted from Gemmen Wilson, "Calling on the Saints," 50–51.

"But neither" she adds, "did the church"—the living church, the *as if it were true* church, the *as if it were real amid the all too real* church.

She says, "While the church may have been partly responsible for encouraging me to live and work in the inner city, I never blamed the church for the rape. I do, however, 'blame' it for my recovery. Not that recovery came easily."

Recovery may not have come easily, but it came with words and actions we probably recognize: hot casseroles lovingly prepared, church folk mowing the lawn, offers for babysitting and housecleaning. Words like, "I love you," and "you are one of us," and "we are in this with you"7—words and actions surrounding her, dare I say it, like a great cloud of witnesses, flooding the world of the all too real with demonstrations of fellowship and healing and hope based on God's living love, enacted love, deeply felt love.

As if it were true.

Love.

I hesitated to share Heather's story. For one, even now, I'm not sure my gender can speak of rape with integrity, since all too often my gender, men, have been the agents of rape. When my gender speaks of a rape victim's "recovery" we risk sounding glib. So I wonder about that. I guess that's why I've used her words more than not.

But there's another thing, too, maybe even more fundamental than questions of gender: her courage is not only beyond my grasp, it's beyond anything anyone, male or female, would *choose* to grasp.

Her faith speaks to an "assurance of things hoped for" and, perhaps even more mysteriously, a "demonstration of things not seen."

Maybe your presence here today is somewhat mysterious to you as well—a demonstration of things not seen.

And maybe, if we thought about it, we might have someone to blame, too.

To blame for wholeness when we had every right to be broken.

To blame for peace when we had every right to rage.

To blame for love when we had every right to hate.

To blame for forgiveness when we had every right to bitterness.

Sometimes it happens that way, as we sing and pray, as we look to Jesus, only looking not for someone to blame but for someone to praise, indeed looking for the One Hebrews calls the pioneer and perfecter of our faith—and somehow it seems as if it were real, as if the promise of Christ was demonstrated, is being demonstrated, and shall be demonstrated.

Waters part.

Strength is won out of weakness.

Joy out of sorrow.

Courage from fear.

As if it were true.

As if it were dry land.

May it be so for all of us.

In the name of the Father, the Son, and the Holy Spirit. Amen.

January 5, 2009

12

Dancing in the Desert

Preaching in a chapel setting is not wholly unlike congregational preaching, particularly as it addresses the sometimes divisive events that negatively affect the community of faith. I wrote the sermon below during a time of turbulence, both in the United States and locally. Nationally, we were seeing the criminalization of Muslims and the forging of a war policy that had neither boundaries nor limits. But it was not only that the world was (and at the time of my writing, still is) in turmoil: theological education often feels more like ghettoes of conflict than a community that is united in its diversity.

Walking onto a seminary campus in America can be like walking into a field of warring groups, their signs and respective turf marked out. Crossing boundaries of ethnicity, gender, sexuality, or theological-political orientation is difficult in the best of times but in our time of polarized politics it is often a harrowing journey—and some, frequently those of color or those whose sexuality is not blessed or whose politics depart from the norm, do not survive the seminary experience.

Seminary, in this setting, can seem like a battleground, where there is only room for one story, the story of my experience, my sexuality, my theological tribe. In this respect, seminary resembles all too well the larger culture of American political discourse.

Samuel Proctor wrote somewhere that the world is full of analysis and dispute, but the faithful pastor is responsible to provide a unique witness to the kingdom of God in the pulpit, to see through the smoke-filled, battered landscapes of controversy for a clear sign of God's presence. No one, says Proctor, can replace that invaluable witness in the life of the church, and the same can be said for the seminary.

While church and seminary have a common need for this kind of prophetic witness, the two settings, the Lord's Day and the weekly worship offered during the academic term, are different in pronounced ways. Chapel preaching, for example, does not belong to one professor or one camp in the community, but to the whole seminary community. Additionally, the seminary chapel is often the "public face" of the theological community, where guest lecturers and preachers speak as well as the location in which shared worship can take place. For example, on the particular day when this sermon was given, we were sharing worship with our sister school, Wartburg Theological Seminary. As a community, our seminary was in the process of assessing our life together as a community that is at once united and diverse. At any time, then, this sort of conversation is one that requires restraint, discernment, and humility.

Given the complexity of seminary community, chapel preaching has a collaborative quality—there is really no such thing as a responsible "lone ranger" in the pulpit. In fact, this sermon was situated within a collaborative effort. Through the prayerful guidance of chapel leaders, community worship became a place where people of color could testify to the way the Spirit works within their communities, making public their lament, their prophetic witness to the majority culture, as well as their gifts to God in worship. It is this service that I refer to as taking place "next week," an "unscripted event of Pentecost;" the service was led by two women, one African American and the other Ojibwa.

DANCING IN THE DESERT

Thus says the Lord, *your Redeemer, the Holy One of Israel: For your sake I will send to Babylon and break down all the bars, and the shouting of the Chaldeans will be turned to lamentation. I am the* Lord, *your Holy One, the Creator of Israel, your King. Thus says the* Lord, *who makes a way in the sea, a path in the mighty waters, who brings out chariot and horse, army and warrior; they lie down, they cannot rise, they are extinguished, quenched like a wick: Do not remember the former things, or consider the things of old. I am about to do a new thing; now it springs forth, do you not perceive it? I will make a way in the wilderness, and rivers in the desert. The wild animals will honor me, the jackals and the ostriches; for I give water in the wilderness, rivers in the desert, to give drink to my chosen people, the people whom I formed for myself so that they might declare my praise. (Isa. 43:14–21)*

Six days before the Passover Jesus came to Bethany, the home of Lazarus, whom he had raised from the dead. There they gave a dinner for him. Martha served, and Lazarus was one of those at table with him. Mary took a pound of costly perfume made of pure nard, anointed Jesus' feet, and wiped them with her hair. The house was filled with the fragrance of the perfume. But Judas Iscariot, one of his disciples (the one who was about to betray him), said, "Why was this perfume not sold for three hundred denarii and the money given to the poor?" (He said this not because he cared about the poor, but because he was a thief; he kept the common purse and used to steal what was put into it.) Jesus said, "Leave her alone. She bought it so that she might keep it for the day of my burial. You always have the poor with you, but you do not always have me." (John 12:1–8)

One gets the sense that the people to whom the prophet preached knew the desert like some of our ancestors knew the land during the Dust Bowl: it seemed as if the desert that surrounded them would go on forever, that its power, like its thirst, was unquenchable. It is tempting at this point to talk about the desert of the soul, long a favorite stomping ground of preachers. We never tire of talking about the desert in our spiritual lives, in our prayer lives, in our walk with Jesus, in our three years of seminary that seem more like forty years.

There is a time for that kind of preaching. And, what is more, there are probably a few here who would say "Amen" to that particular sermon. And, so encouraged, I might even engage in a little "rhythmic grumbling" for our mutual edification and collective enjoyment. I might even prefer that kind of preaching, but not today.

Not today because I can't. Instead, it seems to me Isaiah would have us attend not only to the deserts of our hearts, but also the deserts of our social realities. Isaiah would want us to know that the two are inextricably linked. Which is to say, whatever else the Babylonian exile was, it was not just an occasion for a little spiritual mentoring, a little "How goes it with your soul?" kind of situation. It was a social reality that had turned a chosen nation into the disconnected, fractured social reality of the refugee and asylum seeker. The Babylonian exile dried up human dignity and humanity more unmercifully than the fiercest, hottest of suns.

But it is not only Isaiah that compels me. There is another reason, an east wind, a troubling wind, a wind churning up the dusts of a broken humanity, it is this wind that has taken my tongue captive, parching the word I would speak, with the word I must speak . . . a word about deserts and wildernesses.

Like deserts we have heard and wildernesses we have known.

Like Israel had known. It was not only the physical reality of desert that surrounded them in exile, but it was the desert of the past, the desert of the slave memory, of bondage in the house of Pharaoh. And that desert memory grew tighter, like a noose around the neck, in the desert experience of Babylonian exile.

There was the cosmic context, the contest that went on without ceasing, contests between Yahweh and the gods, Israel and the nations. And in that contest, the gods and the nations thundered with armies and warriors, chariots and horses—all while the desert of the word seemed only to grow deeper, more pervasive, more undeniable.

And around them everywhere the desert grew.

Deserts grew like the ones we know:

The desert of a "global war on terror," a war that has no boundaries, no end, no real beginning.

A war that would make every citizen a potential terrorist and every Muslim a fanatic.

A war that is fed by not by necessity, but by fear.

Deserts like the ones we see in Dubuque, where crack houses and poverty combine to create isolation and desolation.

Deserts like the ones we see here and beyond, where a culture of racism not only exists, but seems to grow in stature, claiming its victims, naming its victories, writing its history.

And there are others, too, some from distant places, but its breath reaches us even here, even through the soft-spoken testimony of Samuel Peni.

If you have an opportunity to speak to him, he will tell you about his home in the Sudan, as he did at our home not long ago.

Since talking to Samuel, I've learned that since 1956, Sudan has known just eleven years of peace, the rest, some forty years, has been nothing but war. And it has brought a death toll of "at least 2.5 million and the displacement of more than half the entire population of southern Sudan." Over half of the nation—a nation of nine million people—has been turned into refugees and asylum seekers as the Islamic North tries to "remake and remold the entire country in its own Arab-Islamic vision . . ."[1]

One leader said it was like trying to rule "over a kingdom of broken eggs. Families scattered, tribes scattered, leaders dead, and traditions broken; how am I supposed to put this back together again?"[2]

To see deserts like this, to see how they grow, the predictable response is despair. The predictable, scripted response is pack up and move on. The script almost demands a loss of hope, a loss of a future, and we would almost be ashamed to do otherwise.

And so we might hear John's Gospel. So we might hear Judas—not as double minded but rational in light of the world's needs. His reaction was in keeping with the script. But Mary's response was different. She knew the desert of poverty and shame as deeply and perhaps more deeply than anyone there, but her response was anything but scripted.

Indeed, it was not the visible act that got Judas's attention, but the fragrance, billowing up like soft, gentle, invisible clouds, surrounding everyone, announcing the song of Mary's tears, weeping on the wilderness weary feet of Jesus, but not for sorrow, but for joy, spilling the everything of her life in worship of the One who had come into the wilderness of our lives. It was as if the tears she shed were the tears of hope that had been brought forth from the otherwise parched land of her world, tears that rejoiced, as waters might rejoice in a desert land.

Perhaps this was the difference between Judas and Mary: Judas saw and responded to the desert, but Mary, who knew the desert, still chose to respond to the Savior who came into the desert with his own life, pouring out his everything, his love, so that our wilderness might become his sanctuary.

So it was that Mary was no longer following the script, no longer compelled by that troubling wind, but lifted by the Spirit that gathered the broken parts of her life into the praise of God's life and love come to us in the fullness of Jesus Christ.

1. Meyer, "Stories from Sudan," 640–41.
2. Ibid., 640.

And so Isaiah brings to us the song of hope that might recall to us the song of Easter, a song that rises early morning, before the dawn: a song that comes to us on the breath of the Spirit, making a way out of no way, turning the "shock and awe" of chariots and horses, warriors and armies, into the silence of the creation, a creation whose once parched, wrinkled skin now trembles with rising waters, bubbling from springs we had not known, coursing through ravines we had not seen, giving drink to the thirsty, giving song to the weary, giving hope to the hopeless.

Maybe it was the Spirit, that wind from God, that moved Augustino Al Nur, like Mary was moved, to follow the Spirit in an unscripted, precipitous, superlative act of hope. Maybe the Spirit is what moved Augustino that day, a hot day in April, an Easter day in 1999, when Augustino, a Sudanese Christian living in the Sudan's northern region, the Muslim-controlled region of the Sudan, began to dance in the desert.

Augustino was sitting alongside his friend, Gabriel Meyer, a poet and journalist, as they celebrated an Easter mass together with other Christians from that community. The scene was scripted, like worship usually is: everyone who had been invited was present; the ceremony was under way; the table was prepared; the words of institution were spoken; the bread was broken, the cup was poured out; the called were invited.

But then something happened, something that had not been planned, someone who had not been invited was coming.

They knew because they could hear the drums announcing someone's coming. Perhaps they wondered, Is this the sound of destruction? Is this the sound of war? After all, they were Christians in a Muslim-controlled region—there was a history between them. Augustino himself bore the scars of that history: the history of how, in another April, in another Easter some fourteen years before, he was arrested and tortured for being a Christian catechist. For four months he was tormented: with ropes, and chains, and beatings, and pliers, and hunger, sleeplessness. He was spit on and humiliated. At the end, the prison guards tied him to the ground in a cross-like formation, a kind of mock crucifixion.

And now, some fourteen years after his escape, Augustino heard the drums, along with his friend Gabriel, and the other Christians there. And perhaps they remembered the desert that surrounded them. And maybe some feared.

Even so, these drums were not the drums of war, but the beginnings of an almost surreal scene, according to Meyer, who described what happened next: "Dressed in traditional Sudanese, they chanted the name Allah, lifting Korans above their heads, moving in a kind of round dance as they saluted their neighbors on the occasion of the Christian feast."[3]

Meyer, who was perhaps as bewildered as he was relieved by what he saw, turned to see how Augustino was reacting. But when he looked for him, he could not find him. Augustino's place was empty. He was not with the other elders, not in the place where he was supposed to be, not in the place that both propriety and history might have prescribed for him. Instead, when Meyer finally saw Augustino, he "was in the middle of the circle dancing there with the Suffi [Muslims]."[4]

Dancing there in the middle of a desert, washing the wilderness of our inhumanity with the deep, strong drumbeat of reconciliation, a sound that rumbles through desert and heart, soul and body, something like the drumbeat sound of doxology.

But deserts are real and this one was no different—a year and a half later, Augustino was assassinated by government officials near his home. But his lasting memory is not his suffering, but his song. Not his death in the desert, but his dance in the midst of it.

All this leads me to wonder whether there was something of the spirit of Augustino with us on Friday night, at our home as we had dinner with Samuel Peni, and listened as he shared his determination to stay in the Sudan. He and the church at Yambio are building a future for the village: Samuel told me that they have one of their number in the second year of medical school, another in training for law, and yet others who will be teachers. As he spoke, he lit up, almost as if light were dancing into the promise of the future, a future that God was opening, a way that God was making for the people of the Sudan.

And what of us? I think there is something of that dance taking place here, too. An unscripted kind of dance, precipitous even. I am told next Tuesday will be Pentecost here at the seminary. It is not Pentecost, of course, but in the sometimes unscripted ways of the Spirit it will be. There will be some dancing in this place next week, some singing that you might not anticipate, some preaching that might surprise you. It's not part of the

---

3. Ibid., 644.
4. Ibid.

script, but it is part of the Lord's way through the wilderness: unscripted, superlative, and even precipitous.[5]

Of course, none of this means that the winds of trouble have disappeared or even eased. The forecast is for more windy weather ahead. Still, what Mary did so many thousands of years ago is a witness to us: One who has made a way out of no way is still palpable in the presence of the Spirit, even today. That witness carries the breath of the Word, a Word that has come, is coming, and shall come into our wilderness with unscripted events of the Spirit, precipitous acts of reconciliation, and superlative demonstrations of hope.

May we join in that dance, a dance to which we have been called. In the name of the Father, and the Son, and Holy Spirit. Amen.

March 20, 2007

---

5. The following Tuesday, Dawn Helton-Anishinaabeqwa performed an Ojibwa smudging ceremony where she "smudged" Native leaders in the UDTS community, acknowledging our work on behalf of Native churches in North America. The ceremony involved the use of smoldering sweet grass, tobacco, and prayer, filling the sanctuary with the fragrance of Native prayers to the Great Spirit.

13

Casting Shadows

THE FOLLOWING SERMON CAME toward the end of the spring semester, during a time when many of our students are actively engaged in the search process; it also came at a time when many of us in the Midwest are breaking into our tool sheds, pulling out rakes, hoes, and packets of seed. In this particular sermon, the former was in the foreground of my mind even as the latter activity dominated my weekend activities. So this sermon, you could say, "grows" out of those two activities. You will see that I attempt to name some of the doubts that accompany our invitation to serve in the local church. At the same time, I wanted to underscore the distinguishing theological impulse that leads us to this kind of work: the doctrine of revelation.

In a sense, without overworking the analogy, I was trying to "cultivate" a particular kind of relationship to the congregation through the analogy of gardening, particularly the community garden. The word *cultivate* is not an inappropriate word for chapel preaching, since, according to George Lindbeck, religious language, and Christian language in particular, is a communal phenomenon.[1] Chapel, in particular, is a place where a community of theologians, students and teachers, comes together to rehearse or perform its "cultural-linguistic" inheritance. Since our word *seminary* comes from the Latin word meaning "nursery" (*seminarium*), it may be reasonable that preaching in such a setting is accented by formative concerns.

It was in this vein that I was intrigued by the letter of 1 John 3:1–2, in particular the way the writer seems to express awe in our name, "that we should be called the children of God," and then a double awe as he

---

1. Lindbeck, *The Nature of Doctrine*, 33.

declares, "for that is what we are." To my ear, that's the tension that many pastors experience in a quite real way, as we preach and pastor to a people who "should" be called the "body of Christ" and indeed, despite considerable evidence to the contrary, really are. And yet, it is difficult not to be unduly influenced by the sentiment that the church ranks pretty low in the world's view of the future. That sentiment was captured in this giddy prediction written for the pages of *The Times* newspaper of London:

> "Surely goodness and mercy shall follow me all the days of my life." I saw the famous words from Psalm 23 on a painting recently, well, as a painting more accurately, because that's all the canvas was, raised white letters on white background.... In any case, this is my prediction for the next big thing art-wise: quotations from the Book of Common Prayer, or the Bible, King James version, on paintings, posters, on T-Shirts, on mugs, on tattoos. As the grip of actual religious belief ever loosens, the language of religion, shorn of any meaning beyond the beauty of the words, will flower.[2]

For those who pastor congregations, it is the close interaction between the biblical witness and congregational life that permits the root to take hold in the soil of our imagination, producing language with meaning. But that interaction between text and context implies even more than interpretive work itself, however important it may be. George Steiner's *Real Presences* reminds us that language without presence is haunted language: "Where God clings to our culture, to our routines of discourse, He is a phantom of grammar...."[3] Luke's language suggests a paradox of communion, for as Christ seems to withdraw further from our earthly life, we are nevertheless bathed in a shadow of promise that lengthens as Christ ascends.

CASTING SHADOWS

See what love the Father has given us, that we should be called children of God; and that is what we are. The reason the world does not know is that it did not know him. Beloved, we are God's children now; what we will be has not yet been revealed. What we do know is this: when he is revealed, we will be like him, for we will see him as he is. (1 John 3:1–2)

Then [Jesus] led them out as far as Bethany, and, lifting up his hands, he blessed them. While he was blessing them, he withdrew from them and was

---

2. Crampton, "The Word Made Art," 20.

3. Steiner, *Real Presences*, 1.

carried up into heaven. And they worshiped him, and returned to Jerusalem with great joy; and they were continually in the temple blessing God. (Luke 24:50–53)

"See what love the Father has given us, that we should be called children of God; and that is what we are."

There's almost a sense of wonder or awe in the way that John begins this chapter. Almost as if he were holding a seed, a hard-edged seed, between thumb and finger, and saying, "All that contained in this little thing! If you didn't know what it was, you'd sweep it up and drop it in the dustbin; if you didn't know what it was, you'd say dust; if you didn't know what it was, you'd say there was no future in it, and certainly no fruit in it. If you didn't know what it was . . ."

Although we are happy to say that, by the grace of God, we do know who we are because we know *whose* we are, we may readily admit to sometimes thinking that what we're about here is too small, too insignificant compared to the kinds of pronouncements that characterize our century. Actually, what we are about may seem less like marching to the tune of a hymn like "Onward Christian Soldiers," and more like the dirge that accompanies those who are left to pick their way through the wreckage of the church's historical decline.

So it seems, at least according to some. God may not be dead in American culture, but some point out that God doesn't exercise the same kind of influence that God enjoyed in the past. Today, in "The End of Christian America," *Newsweek's* Jon Meacham says, "the Christian God is [not] dead, but that [God] is less of a force in American politics and culture than at any other time in recent memory."[4]

Such headlines are eye catching not only because they're big and audacious, which they are, but also because they're speculative—they're making a prognosis about the future, a future in which all the indicators point down.

Despite John's seemingly clear sense that the world and the church see things very differently, it is nevertheless tempting to see ourselves through the speculative lens of the world—it is the all-seeing eye that surrounds us, colonizing our imaginations, so that we can become terribly discouraged in our calling.

4. Meacham, "The End of Christian America," 34.

But today's texts introduce us to a different doctrine, not the doctrine of speculation, the complex calculus by which we determine the future, but, rather, the doctrine of revelation.

To begin with, John takes the seed that is us, our sometimes hard-edged, mean-spirited, unpromising little lives in his hand and says, "See, look, take a gander at the love of the Father! Look how much God has given us that these people, this church, this community should carry the genetic information of God's love in the world!"

John is not trying to boost our self-esteem, as if that might help us overcome the obstacles of the future, that's not his concern at all. John stresses that God has given us this genetic information. We were not, according to John, *born* with it. We may be natural-born killers, to borrow the movie title, but we are not *natural*-born Christians. To put it another way, in John's view, we responded to information from God, information implanted in our hearts and minds so that we might become like Christ.

If you want, maybe we could say God is in the business of genetic engineering or genetic redemption, splicing the genetic information of Christ with the genetic reality of our earthly condition, meshing us with God's love for the world.

John, in keeping with a lot of biblical metaphor for the Christian life, says that the community of faith is born of the seed of God. God's own life is implanted in the soil of our earthly lives.

That might be a particularly rich metaphor, especially for those of us who are called to pastor in sometimes unpromising places.

Like, for example, the bins where we grow vegetables in our backyard, which not so long ago were more characterized by compost than creation. But it happens, every spring, around this time, for reasons I find difficult to decipher, I plant seeds in that unpromising soil, and something comes over me: ground that I was once indifferent to, after I plant, it becomes a place I return to, again and again. Before it was just clay, mostly. Stick-to-your-boots clay. Not much use for it except maybe for a lawn.

But after I drop a few seeds into the soil, I wake up early in the morning, and I look, sometimes the very next day, half hoping to see the slender shoot of a future bursting through the topsoil of the present.

Of course, I know it's too early for the seed to have germinated, but I go anyway, almost prayerfully, anticipating the future, even imagining it. I see the future, tender lettuces, butternut squash, and even eggplants that I don't like very much; I imagine the roasted vegetable medleys that will fill our kitchen with aromas of feasting; I imagine the delight of digging up potatoes out of the ground in August, marveling that all these spuds have been buried like hidden treasure, waiting to be discovered.

Perhaps that is why John speaks of us with wonder, saying we do not know what we shall be—this has not been revealed, but when it is revealed, we shall be as Christ is, for we will see Christ as he is.

When we respond to God's call, going where God sends us, it is okay to listen to speculation about the future. It's there and we can learn from it. It makes no sense to ignore frost warnings. But when we're in the business of making disciples, we go with a sense of confidence.

Like the psalmist, we pray (or plant) in the morning, and then we watch. Go to your callings with a sense of anticipation and let your imagination be guided by God's revelation of completeness in Christ.

But a garden is hard work, and anyone who tells you otherwise is either a liar or never actually had a garden to begin with. There's work to be done. It doesn't just happen. Forming congregations takes a disciplined use of time, attention to detail, and focus of mind.

I remember reading somewhere that the sign of a healthy garden is the shadow of the gardener.

Every one of us has been given a place in the garden of the church. And I would say that the church is a community garden in which we all have something to grow in each other. It's not modern agriculture, creating monocultures for profit. The church is more like a community garden, the kind of garden you sometimes see in the inner city, it's diverse, it's eclectic, it's personal, it's public, and, if you're a type-A personality, it's going to drive you crazy, but a good kind of crazy. Here in the community garden of the church, all of us have an opportunity to build up our neighbor in the love of Christ. So, cast your shadow in this place, cast your shadow of compassion and care on those around you, cast your shadow of prayer on those who grieve, cast your shadow.

Back in Luke, Jesus cast a shadow that was unmistakable. They thought they were seeing a ghost of the past but what they saw, or, rather, what was *revealed* to them, was the Christ of the past, present, and future. Christ cast a shadow over that community—a shadow of living promise.

Perhaps also, as he lifted up his hands in blessing, ascending into heaven, his shadow fell upon them again, as it by God's grace falls on us even now.

The shadows of the economy, the shadows of success or failure, they are part of our lives and we can learn from them. They are, if you will, the frost warnings that come our way from time to time. But they should never define us. After all, we were planted in the shadow of the cross, a shadow that illumines this present darkness with an everlasting light. Amen.

April 28, 2009

14

Breathing Patterns

As I look at my preaching of the past couple years, both in the seminary and in the local church, I seem to speak of fear more frequently than in the past. I do not know if the world is a more fearful place than it was twenty years ago or whether I have simply grown more sensitive to the winds of trouble as I have aged. Either way, students who are finishing their academic work and preparing to enter the pastorate may feel a world of trouble closing in on them, even overshadowing the celebrative events of graduation and ordination.

I suppose that is what struck me about the occasion for this sermon: its celebrative quality. I have grown attached to the baccalaureate service because, unlike the larger graduation ceremony, the baccalaureate takes place in our chapel, a close and familiar setting where we, as a community, have witnessed our students grow, struggle, and ultimately, by God's grace and a lot of hard work, receive calls to serve as pastors. And it seems to me that this service in particular is festive and joyful—students and faculty and seminary staff singing with gusto one last time together before the paths of calling take them in their different directions. People smile more easily, laugh more freely, rejoice more robustly amid the memories and sound of fellowship in chapel.

But the text assigned by the daily lectionary was out of sync with our celebrative mood. It spoke of the disciples in a hideout, doors locked and windows shuttered. Despite our appropriate sense of rejoicing, it struck me that the picture of the church given to us by John was more true to reality than the pride or sense of confidence we were experiencing amid the graduation celebration. It also seemed to say out loud what we might be embarrassed to say in such a celebrative context: that the world, and the church, is awash in fear and perhaps even entombed in it. By contrast, John's way of describing Jesus' coming and the gift of the Spirit suggests that we, like the disciples, have been caught up in God's new creation, a creation that takes our breath away even as it gives us the breath of the Spirit for the everlasting praise of the Triune God.

BREATHING PATTERNS

When it was evening on that day, the first day of the week, and the doors of the house where the disciples had met were locked for the fear of the Jews, Jesus came and stood among them and said, "Peace be with you." After he said this, he showed them his hands and his side. Then the disciples rejoiced when they saw the Lord. Jesus said to them again, "Peace be with you. As the Father has sent me, so I send you." When he said this, he breathed on them and said to them, "Receive the Holy Spirit. If you forgive the sins of any, they are forgiven them; if you retain the sins of any, they are retained." (John 20:19–23)

Breathe, breathe, thank God Almighty, you can breathe at last! It's been three, four, maybe even five years of trying to catch your breath between waves of exams, and oceans of papers, and apparently infinite reading assignments. And it's been hard, to say the least. But today it's different: you're graduates and today you can breathe. Truth is, all of us are breathing little more easily today. You can tell we're feeling better by the way we sing the hymns: which is to say, we're singing them, not mumbling our way through them. What's more, instead of disguising our voices, the organ compliments our singing and that's always a good sign.

Everything about today,

>from your teachers to those who have come to support you,

Everything about today says you can breathe easily . . .

Well, almost everything about today says you can breathe, everything except for our reading from John.

John's image of the church, John's *after-the-resurrection, after-graduation church,* suggests a church in hiding rather than the church on fire; a church in a muddle rather than the church on a mission—an image none too encouraging.

The disciples, John tells us, had locked the doors for fear of the Jews. We might conclude that Jews were to be especially feared, but that's not supported by the text. To begin with, they themselves, the disciples, were Jews. They did not fear themselves, obviously, so reading this in a coarsely antisemitic light casts their behavior in the wrong light. Nevertheless, they did fear persecution by people from their own tribe. Moreover, John's word choice here is important: the disciples, John tells us, had locked the doors for fear, for *phobon*, of the Jews. John uses coinage we recognize in our own language, *phobia*, a root we attach to describe a host of irrational fears:

 acrophobia (fear of heights),

  xenophobia (fear of foreigners),

   arachnophobia (fear of spiders).

And perhaps, most relevant to today's text, claustrophobia (fear of small spaces). In each case, *phobos*, fear, is more resident in the one doing the fearing than in the reality of the thing feared. More could be said about this, but suffice to say that they, the disciples, were afraid, manic afraid.

 Maybe we know what it's like: fear of recession; fear of terrorism; fear of climate change; fear of the next killer virus. Fear. Even Stephen King, the Master of Scary, complains that these days it's difficult to write stories that are as scary as the evening news.

 And we might be inclined to agree.

 Except it's not simply on the news. It's in our homes, in our places of worship. Fear is in here, in us. We may see the evidence of fear in security fences, but before there was the security fence there was the feeling of threat, the certainty that something ominous was coming our way.

 It's like getting a phone call from your mother, when she doesn't usually call, and she's talking on the other end of the phone, but you know it can't be good, what she's about to say, something in her voice tells you it can't be good. Maybe it's the tenseness in her voice, like she's saving breath for the word that it's going to take her whole life to say. And you hold your breath, you brace yourself, because you know it's coming, the thing feared, the thing run from, the thing any of us would hide from.

 And maybe that's us too. Fear is all around us, and probably most significant, it is deep within us.

 It's coming, we say to ourselves, though not too loudly, it's coming. We might sing the songs of faith, but not too loudly lest our neighbors hear. We might pray, but not with too much hope, lest what little faith remains to us be swept away by what is going to happen anyway. And our preaching? Let it be encouraging, but not prophetic; let it be optimistic, but not evangelistic.

We may have a memory of faith, a memory of courageous witness, but it is elusive to us now. The poet Maryann Corbett speaks to the longing of many of us when she says,

> I want it back, the confidence in air—
>
> *ruah, pneuma, spiritus*—the breath that stirs the vocal chords [of] choirs.[1]

Confidence in air. We may want this confidence in air, but it is as elusive to us as it was to the disciples.

Yet within today's text, something unexpected happens. Something implausible happens. Something that even seems impossible. In spite of all the security features of fear, despite all the locks, the secrecy, the shadows, the hiddenness, in spite of all of this, John reports that this lockdown reality has been totally breached: *breached not by what the disciples knew was coming, but by the One who promised his coming.*

"Jesus came and stood among them."

We don't know how Jesus came; only that he came. We don't know how he got through the barbed-wire fences of fear that coiled around that house; don't know how he "picked" the locks of ecclesial insecurity; don't know how he did it any of it, all we know is that he, the Lord Jesus, came and stood among them.

Jesus stood among them, stands among us, speaking through the marks of the cross but communicating none of the fear of the cross and all of the love of the cross, the love of God.

And the disciples rejoiced when they recognized their Savior . . .

They rejoiced. What's in that little word, "rejoiced"?

Well, we can only imagine what the sound of rejoicing was like in that cramped, claustrophobic, hole-in-the-wall excuse for a church. But maybe it was like the moment when the lost are found, the blind see, and the lame walk . . .

And what about the lame?

The lame, when they are made to walk,

---

1. Corbett, "Prophesying to the Breath," 13.

> they don't just walk, they do the tango,
>> they dance on their toes.
>>> And when they're finished dancing, they leap.
>>>> And just to show off,
>>> they do a headstand,
>>> then they spin around on their pinkies,
>> let their legs swing 'round like windmills.
> And when they're finished leaping, spinning and showing off, they run for the sheer joy of running.
> And when they're finished running, they jump for the sheer joy of jumping.

They jump like a three-year-old jumps, I'm speaking from personal experience, they jump for the sake of jumping, even when they shouldn't jump, *especially* when they shouldn't jump—

> like when you're trying to cross a busy street,
>> and there she is jumping around
>>> like a thirty-pound frog tethered to your arm,
>>>> and all you're trying to do is keep everybody alive,
>>> but she's jumping like it's the first time she's ever jumped in her whole little life,
>> which, in a sense, is probably true.

I imagine that cramped, claustrophobic, hole-in-the-wall excuse for a church, changed all of a sudden—*or rather, I imagine the people inside that cramped, claustrophobic, hole-in-the-wall excuse for a church, changed all of a sudden.*

And if you ask my opinion, Jesus should have left it right there, disciples leaping, spinning, and jumping. But then he goes and pulls a Trinity: "As my Father sent me, so I send you."

And this is the irony of the text: the scariest part of the text is *not* that the disciples were afraid of the Jews or that their fears were real or imagined, but that God in Jesus Christ enters into our fear and calls us to do likewise—

that's the scary part,

the *take your breath away* part,

the *get yourself crucified* part,

the *take up your cross and follow me* part,

the *I'm not sure I can do this* part,

the *let's think about this a little bit longer* part,

the *maybe we ought to form a committee to study this a bit further?* part.

And they were sucking wind. That's why Jesus has to say, "Peace be with you" two times. Because the peace he gives is not the peace that the world gives. The peace of the world, that will get you a gated community. But the peace God gives, well, that will get you a mission.

Fact is, that's one of the invitations of this text:

to unlock the doors that we've locked;

open the windows that we've closed;

tear down the religious ghettoes we've built.

If God is willing to unlock his love for the world in Jesus Christ,

then we are called to unlock our doors—even the doors of our hearts and tongues—for that message.

But we're not finished yet; remember, Jesus just pulled a Trinity. When Jesus breathes on his disciples, we are being reminded of the way in which the Spirit billows, blows, pours into our crowded, congested bodies, breathes into this claustrophobic, hole-in-the-wall excuse for a church the eternal breath of God's love, equipping the saints for ministry. The *willing* become, by God's grace, the *able.*

So, disciples of Jesus Christ, altogether now, take a deep, cleansing, clear, unapologetic breath of grace.

Lord knows, we need it.

Lord knows, *she* needed it.

Paul Coutinho tells her story.

A story of a mother, and a wife, and she was dying.

The doctors predicted it;

her body confirmed it.

At first she was afraid of what she knew was coming.

But then, according to a friend, she had an experience of God.

Even so, her circumstances didn't change:

She was still dying . . . but she changed.

She didn't pray to be healed anymore.

She prayed that her life, even her dying,

would contribute in some way to a cure for others. She prayed to live her life fully,

as faithfully as she could,

one day at a time.

And near the end, when breathing was surely hardest, she asked her husband for a paper and pencil. He thought she was going to write down her will; instead, she wrote down some simple recipes for meals that he could prepare for their children after she was gone.[2]

It's hard to say what it was she experienced in that breathless place, somewhere between living and dying, between courage and fear . . . but whatever it was, it must have been something like confidence in air.

Something like impossible, implausible, unexpected breathing.

So we have received.

So we have been sent.

And so breathe . . .

Breathe like the first time,

like the last time,

to the everlasting glory of God. Amen.

May 9, 2008

---

2. Adapted from Paul Coutinho, S.J., *How Big Is Your God?*, quoted in *Christian Century*, 8.

15

Sound of Sirens

SOME TEXTS LEAVE THE PREACHER CONFUSED or bewildered as to their meaning or their import for a particular day in the life of the community. A doubtful response to the particular meaning of a text is, at least in my experience, not at all unusual. At other times, my grasp of a text may still be opaque but to its opaqueness is added another quality: irritation. I doubt I am alone in this experience either. Texts can sometimes act like nuisances, pestering you with their questions or their oddities, as you swat at them, cursing them or your choice of vocation, wishing one or the other would go away.

And perhaps this is especially tragic, but the texts I listen to, or the texts that I am *condemned* to listen to, are those texts that seem to attack me, arcing across the dullness of my mind with an edge from which I find escape either difficult or impossible. Indeed, short of canceling the preaching date, escape is probably not an option . . . woe unto me. The pericope from Isaiah 59:1–28 (assigned by the daily lectionary) seemed to be this kind of text, as the prophet's words hummed in my ears, a veritable cloud of blood-hungry insects, burrowing deep into my ears, digging into the back of my neck, driving me out of bed at the odd hour, leaving me with the welts of Isaiah's prophetic infection.

At the time of the sermon, the news was rife with the image of Bernard Madoff and Rod Blagovich and the images of Detroit CEOs facing off against the blistering condemnation of Congress, an event of political theater if there ever was one. Perhaps most stunning to me was listening to Alan Greenspan, former chair of the Federal Reserve, testify before Congress, admitting that his belief in the ability of the financial industry to self regulate showed that he had a "flaw" in his worldview. Even as we digested this trillion-dollar "flaw" in Greenspan's worldview, our Congress and new president urged that the crisis we faced was global and threatened to undo the foundation of commerce if not civilization itself. There was (and still is) a sense of the apocalyptic in the air. Yet, even with this, there was a peculiar lack of alarm in our communities, as if the shadows passing across the television screen were from a distant country and not our own.

Within this context, the theological clue for my interpretation of the text came at verses 15b–16a, which was further highlighted by John Calvin's commentary: "[The Lord] saw that there was no one [to save], and was appalled that there was no one to intervene." What struck me was that despite the alarming testimony of the prophet, only the Lord seemed truly conscious of the gravity of the situation. Or in Calvin's interpretation, God made God's own self astonished. So, actually, the word *conscious* is not adequate here—the Lord is alarmed or, perhaps, *visibly marked* by the way human society embraced inequity and injustice as a system, elevating to the level of political philosophy the exploitation of the many for the benefit of an elite few. Recalling Albert Camus's opening words to *The Rebel*, in this new context of systematized terror and exploitation, the act of murder, which was once decried as a horror to humanity, is now elevated into a new law, the law of the global economy: "Once crime was as solitary as a cry of protest; now it is as universal as science. Yesterday it was put on trial; today it determines the law."[1] The inhuman eclipses the human as normative. That may be the "new normalcy" and, as such, it may be immune to question. But the prophet Isaiah, if he is to be heard today, is likely to sound the alarm of God's justice. By God's grace, we will hear and respond.

SOUNDS OF SIRENS

*See, the L*ORD*'s hand is not too short to save, nor his ear too dull to hear. Rather, your iniquities have been barriers between you and your God, and your sins have hidden his face from you so that he does not hear.*

*Justice is turned back, and righteousness stands at a distance; for truth stumbles in the public square, and uprightness cannot enter. Truth is lacking, and whoever turns from evil is despoiled. The L*ORD *saw it and it*

---

1. Camus, *The Rebel*, 3.

> *displeased him that there was no justice. He saw that there was no one, and was appalled that there was no one to intervene; so his own arm brought him victory, and his righteousness upheld him. (Isa. 59:1–28 [1–2, 14–16])*

Perhaps you have had the experience of being in bed, late at night, two or three in the morning when everyone is, or should be, asleep, and you hear a siren in the distance, perhaps you hear several sirens. You listen, but only in a distant way, as sirens in the distance have an almost lazy, indifferent feel to them, invisible companions to a sleepless moment at night.

But maybe, curiously, perhaps that distance narrows, as the sirens grow closer, their urgency tighter, their whine higher pitched, making their way through a complicated maze of midnight streets, closer.

By now you're awake, alert, wondering, almost excitedly, whether in the odd calculus of trouble, whether these emergency vehicles will come near your street, whether their sirens and lights will materialize on a street near your home. But, you know, in your heart, there is no emergency here, and so you stay in your bed, beneath your covers, next to your spouse, safe in your warm nest of anonymity.

But then, quite suddenly, those distant sirens have somehow become near, have now turned into an intrusive, disruptive blazing, flashing, alarm—and squad cars, and the police personnel, and the lights, and the trouble seem to swarm with all the heat and urgency you never really dreamed was coming your way.

That's the way we might experience Isaiah's text this morning, like a distant siren, not visible to us because it seems so alien to us, and yet its flashing lights, its alarm, its urgency makes its ear-piercing, heart-racing way straight into the place where we live—it seems as if Isaiah aims to wake us, to stir us into alarm, a people who expected no alarm, a people who in the great calculus of alarm, expected alarm to wake someone else on some other street, in some other house, in some other church.

But it appears that the prophet's urgency has not to do with someone else, but us. Isaiah arrives at our doorstep, not politely pulling in and quietly turning off the engine, but like police cars coming to a stop, in the road, owning the road, engines running, lights flashing, more back-up on the way, and before we know it, the police, or, in this case, the prophet is thrusting the intrusive beam of his flashlight into the sanctuary we called home.

"You," says the prophet, "you and your sins are the trouble"—six times in the space of three verses, the prophet uses the second person, making it unmistakable that he believes he has found his mark, that he has identified the trouble and the trouble is "you": "Your iniquitous fingers, your muttering, lying lips, your wicked thoughts," you and your sin.

Perhaps we imagine there is a mistake. The prophet has made a mistake. It happens, even to the best of us. It will all be cleared up in the morning.

But, you and I, we are biblical Christians, so we cooperate, we go with the prophet, imagining that all will be well in the morning, the misunderstanding will be cleared up, apologies will be made, and we'll be big about it, and it will be nothing, we will go home, the prophet will go away, find some other neighborhood to haunt, after all that's what prophets do, and we're prophet-abiding people, so we go along, it'll be cleared up in the morning.

But if we were hoping for that to happen, if we were hoping for the prophetic witness of Isaiah to somehow ease up, to turn off the sirens of alarm, we would be disappointed. Alarm is strewn throughout this text. It comes swiftly, unsparingly:

"No one brings suit justly, they rely on empty pleas, they speak lies, they conceive mischief, they beget iniquity."

"Their feet," says prophet, "run to evil, and they rush to shed innocent blood . . ." It almost sounds like a crime of passion, until you get to the next clause: "their thoughts are thoughts of iniquity, and desolation and destruction are in their highways." What we have here is the image of premeditated, systematized, codified crime.

"Their roads are made crooked; no one who walks in them knows peace." And now, "we grope like the blind along a wall, we stumble at noon as in twilight, among the vigorous, as if we were dead."

Needless to say, it's painful to read it, much more so to hear it, and I don't think I need to tell you, least of all you, it's been ugly wrestling with it as a preacher.

Judgment texts are always difficult, almost by definition. Confronted by Godly judgment, we are prone to dodge and duck, to make allowances, offer explanations, or as we like to say in academic circles, to speak of the "complexities" of the situation. That's part of dealing with these kinds of texts, coping with those kinds of interpretive temptations.

But I think that's not the primary problem here—I think the greater burden of this text for me is not so much the judgment it communicates but, rather, our relative lack of alarm in the face of that judgment. We are not alarmed people, by and large. Presbyterians, Methodists, a few Congregationalists scattered in there for good measure. Not known for alarm. Denominations are not built on alarm, neither are pensions. Concerned, perhaps. But alarmed, no, not for the most part.

Even these days, when alarms sound almost hourly, banks collapse daily, jobs disappear by the tens of thousands, over half a million jobs gone in just a month, some of the largest financial scandals in world history, world leaders anxiously trying to quell social unrest, riots, people pouring out into the streets in Eastern Europe.

And it's not like it's so distant anymore; it's here, too. On Sunday, at the church where we worship, a working man, who never makes prayer requests, asked for prayers, as he told us about the forty-two jobs being cut from the company where he works. And prayers like that one are just piled on top of the prayer requests for the son or brother or friend who is being sent on yet another tour of duty, we forget how many they've been on, too many to count, in Iraq or Afghanistan.

With all this going on, it is not our alarm but the conspicuous lack of alarm that is disturbing. Writing in *The New York Times Magazine*, Walter Kirn wonders what has happened to our sense of outrage, moral outrage. He is almost wistful as he yearns for what he calls the good old days of puritanical, finger-wagging hysteria—what the witch trials lacked in due process, he says, they made up for in their capacity to generate a feeling, any kind of feeling that could merit the feeling of threat, the feeling of ominous alarm in the air. And yet . . . and yet, he says, our capacity for alarm, for moral outrage seems to have disappeared just as mysteriously as our 401ks.[2]

We are convinced that the alarm that the prophet sounds is meant for someone else's house, someone else's street, someone else's church. We say to ourselves, it'll all be cleared up in the morning.

But friends, you and I know, God does not sound alarm in vain. God's interventions in human life are never random, never spasmodic, or episodic. God's interventions in our world, God's word which enters into

---

2. Kirn, "The Age of Neo-Remorse," 9–10.

our world with the prophetic siren of justice, and mercy, and peace—that word is always a word on target.

Perhaps more importantly, what is evident in this text, a close reading of this text, is that at the text's existential middle is not so much a report about our lack of responsiveness to God. Our lack of responsiveness is evident, the most predictable thing we see, we are like the dead walking among the vigorous—or we are dead, utterly unresponsive to real, valid, God-centered alarm.

The key that may help us unlock the theological implications of this text comes in verse 16, "The Lord saw that there was no one, and was appalled that there was no one to intervene, so his own arm brought him victory, and his righteousness upheld him." John Calvin, commenting on this verse, notes its peculiar construction, saying that one could render the text as if Isaiah had written, "the Lord was the cause of his own astonishment; as if he had said, "He made himself astonished."[3] Which is to say, what we thought was happening wasn't happening after all. The prophet was not trying to alarm *us*, though alarmed we may be—instead, the prophet was reporting *God's alarm*, an alarm that issues in an interventionist act of inexpressible power and grace.

And this is where we need to check our vocabulary, because when I think of someone who is alarmed, I think of myself and I don't think very clearly or act very effectively when I'm alarmed. My vision turns into a tunnel and I don't see so clearly. But in God's economy, God's astonishment, it does not result in a distortion of God's vision or action, but in a strategic act of intervention that is edgy as well as precise.

I like the image of edgy intervention as a way of talking about God's entrance into our world. If you know anything about interventions, they are awkward things, where false imaginings are confronted by redemptive purposes. An intervention takes time, and it takes community, and it slows things down.

Most of all, it takes love, a love that, like God's own love, is courageous tell it like it is, but even more so, and this is the passion behind it, the power of it, to believe in God's living, active, wondrous grace in the world. To believe in a God-given future—a future so intrusive that we are willing to interrupt business as usual, with a dramatic, edgy intervention inspired by the love of God. I wonder, if the church were to pattern itself with this

---

3. Calvin, *Commentary on the Prophet Isaiah*, 509.

kind of interventionist metaphor, might we be a church that, like the poor sitting on the sidewalks of America or in the gutters of our indifference, might we be a church in the street, determined to make eye contact, to beg, to plead, to insinuate, to be embarrassing, to be awkward, in the way, intervening as a human folly and crazy fool according to the wisdom of the world, but to those who are being saved, the power of God.

Maybe we could become an interventionist church, to be an astonishing church, a church you have to shove aside, trample under, push down, and maybe even crucify.

Brothers and sisters, the alarms of the world are everywhere.

The love of God is here.

Amen.

February 11, 2009

Bibliography

American Indian Consulting Panel. *We May Be Brothers After All: A Position Paper*. United Presbyterian Church in the USA (1972) 29–30.
Augustine of Hippo. *Sermons on the New Testament*. Edited by Edmund Hill and translated by John E. Rotelle. New Rochelle, NY: New City, 1992.
Barth, Karl. *Deliverance to the Captives*. New York: Harper and Brothers, 1961.
Berry, Wendell. *Sex, Economy, Freedom, and Community*. New York: Pantheon, 1992.
———. *The Unforeseen Wilderness: Kentucky's Red River Gorge*. Emeryville, CA: Shoemaker and Hoard, 1991.
———. "Manifesto: The Mad Farmer Liberation Front." In *Good Poems* edited by Garrison Keillor. New York: Viking, 2002.
Blount, Brian K. *Go Preach! Mark's Kingdom Message and the Black Church Today*. Maryknoll, NY: Orbis, 1998.
Brown, Sally. *Cross Talk: Preaching Redemption Here and Now*. Louisville: Westminster John Knox, 2008.
Buber, Martin. *Tales of the Hasidim*. New York: Schocken, 1991.
Burnett III, James H. "Social Issues Luring More Young People into Clergy." *Wisconsin State Journal* May 8 (2007).
Calvin, John. *The Commentaries on the Epistle of Paul to the Hebrews*. Albany: Ages Software, 1996.
———. *Commentary on the Prophet Isaiah: Volume 2*. Albany: Ages Software, 1998.
Camus, Albert. *The Rebel: An Essay on Man in Revolt*. New York: Vintage, 1991 [1956].
Corbett, Maryann. "Prophesying to the Breath." *First Things* May (2008).
Coutinho, Paul, S.J. *How Big Is Your God? The Freedom to Experience the Divine* (Chicago: Loyola, 2007), quoted in "Century Marks," *Christian Century* March 11 (2008): 8.
Craddock, Fred. *Preaching*. Nashville: Abingdon, 1985.
Crampton, Robert. "The Word Made Art." *The Times* 28, July (2009).
Dawn, Marva. *A Royal Waste of Time: The Splendor of Worshiping God and Being Church for the World*. Grand Rapids: Eerdmans, 1999.
Eliot, T. S. "The Dry Salvages." In *Four Quartets*. New York: Harcourt Brace Jovanovich, 1971.
Forde, Gerhard O. *On Being a Theologian of the Cross: Reflections on Luther's Heidelberg Disputation, 1518*. Grand Rapids: Eerdmans, 1997.
Gaventa, Beverly Roberts. *Our Mother Saint Paul*. Louisville: Westminster John Knox, 2007.

Hewett, James Allen. *New Testament Greek: A Beginning and Intermediate Grammar.* Peabody, MA: Hendrickson, 1986.

Hoge, Dean, and Jacqueline E. Wenger. *Pastors in Transition: Why Clergy Leave Local Church Ministry.* Grand Rapids: Eerdmans, 2005.

Intrator, Sam M. *Stories of the Courage to Teach: Honoring the Teacher's Heart.* San Francisco: Jossey-Bass, 2002.

Kilborn, Peter T. *Next Stop, Reloville: Life Inside America's New Rootless Professional Class.* New York: Times Books/Henry Holt, 2009.

Kirn, Walter. "The Age of Neo-Remorse." In *The New York Times Magazine* 25, January (2009).

Kleinfield, N. R. "Through the Cracks, Then Through the Ice: Never Reported Missing, A Honduran Met His Fate in a Brooklyn Lake." In *The New York Times* 1, February (2004).

Lewis, C. S. *The Problem of Pain.* New York: MacMillan, 1947.

———. Learning in War Time. *A sermon preached in the Church of St. Mary the Virgin, Oxford, Fall, 1939.* On line: http://www.calvin.edu/~pribeiro/DCM-Lewis-2009/Lewis/learning%20in%20wartime.doc.

Lincoln Hall (climber). On line: http://en.wikipedia.org/wiki/Lincoln_Hall_(climber).

Lindbeck, George A. *The Nature of Doctrine: Religion and Theology in a Postliberal Age.* Philadelphia: Westminster, 1984.

Lischer, Richard. *The End of Words: The Language of Reconciliation in a Culture of Violence.* Grand Rapids: Eerdmans, 2005.

Marsden, George M. "The Soul of the American University: An Historical Overview." In *The Secularization of the Academy*, edited by George M. Marsden and Bradley J. Longfield. New York: Oxford University Press, 1992.

Meacham, Jon. "The End of Christian America." *Newsweek* 153 (2009) 34-38.

Merrill, Christopher. *The Old Bridge: The Third Balkan War and the Age of the Refugee.* Minneapolis: Milkweed Editions, 1995.

Merton, Thomas. *The Way of Chuang Tzu.* New York: New Directions, 1969.

Meyer, Gabriel. "Stories from Sudan." *Vital Speeches of the Day* 72 (2006) 638-44.

Moltmann, Jürgen. *The Crucified God: The Cross of Christ as the Foundation and Criticism of Christian Theology.* Minneapolis: Fortress, 1993.

Native American Consulting Committee of the United Presbyterian Church in the USA. *Mending the Hoop: Results of Research by the Indian Church Career Project* (Summary). United Presbyterian Church in the USA, 1974.

Neihardt, John G. *Black Elk Speaks: Being the Life Story of a Holy Man of the Oglala Sioux.* Lincoln: University of Nebraska Press, 1932.

Neimöller, Martin. "Grace." In *Against Torture* edited by Allan A. Boesak and Edmond Perret. Geneva: World Alliance of Reformed Churches, 1987.

Old, Hughes Oliphant. *Themes and Variations for a Christian Doxology: Some Thoughts on the Theology of Worship.* Grand Rapids: Eerdmans, 1992.

Rifkin, Jeremy. *Entropy: A New World View.* New York: Viking, 1980.

Rosman, Artur. "Acquainted with the Night: The Art of Jerzy Nowosielski." *Image: Art, Faith, Mystery* 61 (2009) 31-40.

Scarry, Elaine. *The Body in Pain: The Making and Unmaking of the World.* New York: Oxford University Press, 1985.

Steinbeck, John. *East of Eden.* New York: Penguin, 2002.

Steiner, George. *Real Presences.* Chicago: University of Chicago Press, 1989.

Thompson, James W. *Preaching Like Paul: Homiletical Wisdom for Today*. Louisville: Westminster John Knox, 2001.
Tisdale, Leonora Tubbs. *Preaching as Local Theology and Folk Art*. Minneapolis: Fortress, 1997.
Wainwright, Geoffrey. *Doxology: The Praise of God in Worship, Doctrine, and Life*. New York: Oxford University Press, 1980.
Wilson, Heather Gemmen. "Calling on the Saints." *Christianity Today* February (2008) 50–51.
Winterson, Jeanette. "In Praise of the Crack-Up." *The Wall Street Journal Digital Network* 17, October (2009), Life and Style section. On line: http://online.wsj.com/article/SB10001424052748704322004574475654003711242.html
Yeats, William B. "The Second Coming." In *Selected Poems and Two Plays of William Butler Yeats*. New York: Collier, 1962.